REFLECTIONS

OF

RAF WARMWELL

REVISED EDITION

Anthony Cooke

Published by RAF Warmwell Preservation Group

Published by:
RAF Warmwell Preservation Group
26 Fosse Green
Dorchester Dorset
DT1 2RR

First Published in August 2000
Revised in June 2004

Printed by: Creeds the Printers, Broadoak, Bridport, Dorset DT6 5NL

Front cover: Photographs and paintings from author's collection.

Back cover: Pilots of 152 Squadron overlaid with plate from Sgt. Shepperd's crashed Spitfire.

Technical assistance from Bird Computer & Technological Services.

Contents

4   Preface

5   Memories and Reminiscences

38   152 Squadron - Battle of Britain Roll of Honour

40   Roll of Honour of Fatalities – 1 April 1941

History of RAF Warmwell

41   The Road to War

48   The Battle and Beyond

56   1941

60   Wing Operations

63   A New Squadron

65   Operation Jubilee

66   First Americans

68   Of Whirlwinds and Typhoons

75   Station 454, USAAF Moreton

79   D-day, 6 June 1944

81   17 and 14 APCs

84   A Search for Answers:

89   The Death of Sgt. Edmund Shepperd, 152 Squadron

90   The Rubel Memorial

97   Ivan Mason

99   Profile of a Battle of Britain Pilot: Ralph Wolton

107   RAF Warmwell Memorial Appeal

110   "I'll Never Forget Her"

111   RAF Units present at RAF Warmwell

112   Station Defence 1940 - 1944

113   RAF Warmwell Preservation Group

Preface

This second edition continues to be a tribute to RAF Warmwell, a subject that I have lived with since I purchased in the early 1960s a copy of Richard Collier's "Eagle Day – the Battle of Britain".

Since then, my reference library has grown in stature and I have made many friends and probably been in contact with approaching one thousand people who served at Warmwell in an effort to record their personal reminiscences. What began as an interest has become an obsession. Nevertheless, such a project can only be conducted with the help of one's family. Carol, my long suffering wife, has had to endure much and became a 'grass widow' to my preoccupation with the historic events surrounding Dorset's only fighter station.

The history of RAF Warmwell is the history of the people who served there. It is people who make history – the men and women who, of all service branches and many nations, bought with their bodies and minds the freedom we readily accept today without a thought. They were young once, full of confidence and lived for the day; because 'today' literally might have been the last day of their lives.

Today, they are old and frail, their bodies and minds are still paying the price of that conflict over half a century ago. I ask you to remember them, their yesterdays bought us our tomorrow. Their legacy is our freedom.

The anecdotal stories related between these pages is quoted verbatim from the material veterans have supplied. Their words describe the events they experienced.

To everyone who has helped and assisted me over the years I can only express my thanks for your kindness, time and effort. I hope you will not feel it was wasted.

Meanwhile, the work continues.

Anthony Cooke

Memories and Reminiscences

1937-1940

Sandra Stabler spent her early childhood in Crossways, she has distinct and colourful recollections of the airfield being commissioned and of the Empire Air Day displays.

"One of my earliest memories of the presence of the RAF in our village is of standing just outside my parents' shop – now known as Tree Stores in Warmwell Road, but at that time just called "Stabler's" or "the Post Office" – waiting for the arrival of THE BAND! This "big" event was obviously to mark the official opening of Warmwell Airfield. The year was 1937 so I would have been about five years old.

I recall feeling so excited as we had been told that THE BAND would be playing and marching up the road from the station. Together with my brother, Michael, and my sister, Jill, I waited for what seemed at least an hour but was probably only ten minutes for THE BAND to appear in the distance. We kept running into the road, to see if we could see it. There was, fortunately, very little traffic on the roads in those days. At long last we could hear as well as see it coming. I remember being enthralled by the sight of the uniforms, the shiny instruments and the band master looking so important.

Another highlight was the Empire Day Air Display. (We still had an Empire in those days and were given a half day holiday from school.)

We were taken by my parents to watch a display of bi-planes performing aerobatics, and dropping baskets of eggs by parachute. All quite wonderfully exciting to a young child.

The RAF Warmwell Band march through Crossways toward the camp.
Photo: Cooke.

With the declaration of war, life was never the same again and Crossways was caught up in the dramas which took place in the skies over the village."

Sandra Sewell, Crossways Resident

The store would eventually become the YMCA hostel (AC).

*****

Vic Pullen has vivid memories of life in Crossways prior to the war. His recollections describe the security that surrounded Warmwell as war became a reality; the construction of an air raid shelter in the garden and 'life' around the shelter constructed at Moreton railway station.

"Mother, Father, brothers Tony & Graham and myself, lived at Dick o' th' Banks Road for many years before the war started in 1939. My father was an ex-RAF man, employed by the RAF at Warmwell camp and was a sergeant in the local Home Guard. I think it was a unit mainly for the camp or it may have been a part of the Woodsford unit. The reason I think it was based at the Camp is that there are quite a few Crossways people in the photograph supplied and their HQ was at the Camp.

When war started all the roads leading into the camp had pill boxes and barriers across and manned by RAF Police. All families had special passes to get in and out of the village.

Warmwell Camp became a very busy fighter station. They soon found that there was not enough room for all the crews to live on camp and so many families were asked to take

Woodsford Home Guard Unit at RAF Warmwell.
Back row: Bill Dorymead, ?, Don Trevett. Middle row: Tommy Farr, Merv Knight, ?, ?, ?, ?.
Front row: Sgt. Ted Pullen, ?, ?, Sid Keats.
Photo: Pullen

in some the crews in Dick o' th' Banks Road. I can remember Mother taking in about two crewmen at a time, because my brother and I had to give up our room!"

-oOo-

"When the war started, most families had their own air raid shelter in the back garden. I can remember helping my father dig out the big hole – it was about 10ft (2.5m) deep and about the size of a normal room. We then put railway sleepers on the top, and covered these with the dirt we had dug out. We dug steps out to go down into it and hung a curtain across the entrance. We kitted it out with chairs and blankets and torches to provide light. After a while we had a tilley lamp. We used to spend night after night down in the shelter and always went there when the camp siren sounded.

After a time, most families were issued with a Morrison shelter which was made of steel and it was put together in one of the rooms inside the house, but we liked the outside shelter best.

I can remember a few air raids in the day time but I recall one very clearly. It was about 8.15 a.m. and we had just left home to walk to school at Moreton, when the siren sounded. We saw three German bombers come in very low over where the football pitch is today in Dick o' th' Banks Road. We dived into the gorse bushes and the planes passed on over the camp. Spitfires took off and chased them back towards the coast."

-oOo-

"There was a very big shelter at Moreton Station and every evening at about 8 p.m. we all went to this shelter; the women sat inside knitting and chatting; the children played and the men hung around outside chatting and smoking. If no sirens went during the evening we would all troop off home to bed at about midnight – it almost became a way of life.

I do remember that RAF Warmwell had a first class football team – including some top players who had joined the RAF – my father often refereed matches for them."

Vic Pullen, MBE, Wartime Crossways Resident (Broadmayne, Dorset)

The 1939 Woodsford/Warmwell football team was "All conquering" frequently beating most service teams which it played against.
Cooke/McCaughtey

*****

In the early days Woodsford/Warmwell was without a fully operational sick bay, just two orderlies to attend to the medical requirements of the entire camp. Should a doctor be required the services of a medical practitioner was requested from Dorchester.

Aircraftsman 1st Class Mitchell arrived to find the sick bay unit contained six beds and accommodation for the three attendants who had to provide for themselves. In November the station received its first medical officer, F/L (Dr.) Williams.

As Woodsford became fully operational accidents began to occur. The sick quarters staff, aided by some civilian drivers, manned the ambulance and attended all accidents – whether on or off the camp.

On 18 March 1938 Fairy Swordfish K5985 from the Torpedo Training Unit, Gosport, was flying in low cloud and mist and crashed near Swyre. A/C Mitchell was adamant that the incident happened near Lyme Regis but crash reports appear to indicate that it happened in the Purbeck region of Dorset. At the time of writing the actual location has still to be determined but A/C Mitchell's descriptions of the event are worth recording here as it is an example of the problems experienced by the recovery team.

"We were dispatched to a Swordfish crash which hit the cliffs. It was impossible to get the ambulance down to the beach so we had to scramble down the cliff, edging our way to the bottom, then, after releasing the bodies of the crew we had to manhandle them to the top of the cliff; which turned out to be much more difficult than we imagined. Relieved, we made the summit of the cliff and loaded the ambulance and returned to Warmwell, where last rites were performed on the naval airmen."

The crew was actually RAF personnel. P/O F. Williams RAF, Clp C. Coles and LAC D. Hurrell perished in the accident.

Not all the accidents over the ranges were fatal, however. On 25 May 1938 P/O Hunter of 9 FTS (Flying Training School), a bulky amateur boxer, was forced to abandon Hawker Fury K8223 over the Chesil Range.

"I well recall the day I was sent to collect P/O Hunter, his aircraft had collided with a towed target and caught fire. The officer was a large man and had some difficulty in extracting himself from the aircraft but baled out safely and landed in the sea, from where he was rescued. Being an amateur heavyweight boxer he caused the crew of the rescue launch (from 37 Marine Craft Unit Lyme Regis) to struggle as they lifted him from out of the sea. We collected him from the quay at Lyme Regis and brought him back to Warmwell after giving him a check over."

AC Mitchell, Sick Bay, RAF Woodsford 1937/38

*****

Conditions at Warmwell in the early days and months of the war were far from ideal – almost primitive – especially regarding accommodation. The hutments were often unfinished or damp and fuel for stoves was non-existent. There was no hot water in the billets but this was provided in the ablution block, which was often a far walk from one's hut. Many of the camp's regular staff were billeted off the station in requisitioned properties or lodged with local families, often occupying garages as billets.

Like so many young men of the time, twenty-three year old George Barley enlisted in the RAF Volunteer Reserve in May 1939. Over the next few months he attended evening instructional sessions at the local HQ in Beverley Road, Hull and participated in air familiarisation flights from a local aerodrome at Brough, near to Hull. As aircrew, he was given the rank of Leading Aircraftsman and was trained as a wireless operator/air gunner for future service in Bomber Command.

When war was declared, George Barley was called up to full time service. Over the next few days he received his full issue of kit and was soon posted to Prestwick, Scotland, to attend a wireless operators' course. Till then, his instruction had been a mixture of theoretical and practical lectures but had not included live firing. In the first week of January 1940 he, with other trainees from the course, was posted to 10 Bombing & Gunnery School, Warmwell, to attend an air gunnery course.

"We travelled from Scotland by train, arriving late in the evening of either January 3rd or 4th, - we were posted to Warmwell to be trained as air-gunners. We collected our sheets and blankets and was billeted in a Nissen hut, it appeared that at that time no other persons had been living in the Nissen for some time. We were about a week without heating due to there being no coal available – not for us anyway, so we were issued after complaining of the cold with an extra blanket! The heating was done by a coke fire stove which was situated in the centre of the hut.

"Warmwell was then No. 10 Bombing & Gunnery School. Gun training consisted of lectures and flying - we were lectured on aircraft recognition also air-reconnaissance. This being so that we would be able to recognize enemy aircraft at a distance, this was done by showing films and photos of enemy aircraft in flight, head on, side and front view. This was because we were being trained to be air-gunners in bombers (and) *we were taught to operate, strip, clear stoppages and everything about a gun. The guns we were trained on were Vickers Gas Operated and Lewis guns. My instructor was a civilian called Mr. Jones, I seem to recollect that Mr. Jones was an ex-Navy man.*

"Our training hours was from 8 a.m. to 5:30 p.m. with a break for lunch, with one day off per week. I did my first training in an aircraft using a camera gun, this I did twice then started firing a Vickers Gas Operated and Lewis guns. Our air training was carried out by firing at a drogue using live ammunition, this involved two aircraft, one towing the drogue, the other aircraft which the trainee fired the gun from."

The drogue targets were streamed out from the Westland Wallace aircraft operated by the Drogue Towing flight. Each Wallace carried three drogues and would 'string out' a single target which could accommodate a number of trainees firing at the drogue, albeit some considerable distance behind and at an angle to the towing aircraft. The expended ammunition was tipped in coloured ink or dye, which left behind a trace if the rounds of ammunition passed through the canvas drogue. The hits were counted and the score passed by landline to Warmwell after the drogue was detached from the Wallace to fall into a field near Langton Herring, adjacent to the Chesil Range. The exercises required the trainee to fire at the drogue either at the same height as the towing aircraft or from above or below and to the left and right of the towing Wallace.

"We did our air firing practically every day. The two aircraft flying at the same height, higher than the drogue towing aircraft etc. In order that you did not shoot your own aircraft's tail off the mounting of the gun would not rotate a full circle, when facing the tail it would lift up and fire over the tail.

"When dropped the drogue was examined to check on how many bullets had hit the drogue - the air-gunner was informed how good or bad his air firing was, usually after the squad had finished air firing. I qualified as an air-gunner on 10 February 1940 and was then posted to RAF Upwood on Blenheims."

LAC George Barley 10 Bombing & Gunnery School.

George Barley completed 18 sorties, flying in three aircraft types (Wallace, Hind and Harrows) over the Chesil Range, adding 14 hours and 50 minutes to his flying log for the attachment. On 20 January he flew a thirty-five minute sortie with Sgt. A. W. Kearsey. In September, Kearsey was posted to 152 Squadron and fought in some of the earnest combats of the Battle of Britain.

*****

Battle of Britain

Sgt. R W Wolton was on leave when he received a telegram instructing him to make his way to Warmwell to immediately re-join 152 Squadron, the squadron having been transferred from Acklington to Dorset. He relates the events of July 25th, his first combat encounter. Flying with two other pilots in his section, the trio were to destroy a Dornier 17; and he further claimed a Junkers JU 87 shot down.

"P/O Holmes led the section to which I was assigned. Holmes banked and made a pass at the Hun aircraft and seconds later I followed him in. The Dornier came into my gunsights and I pressed the firing button. My Spitfire shuddered under the recoil of its armament as I watched my tracer ammunition strike home. Fractions of a second later I had passed my quarry, and as I pulled out of my attack I was to the south of a group of Junkers JU 87 Stuka dive-bombers. Although my ammunition had hit the DO 17 there was no outward sign that it had caused any real damage.

(The Dornier crashed at Fleet near Weymouth.)

"It looked like the Stukas were about to attack their target, so I made a banking turn and began my pursuit. My diving attack caused them to scatter and I latched onto one of their number and fired the remainder of my ammunition at him. Smoke began to trail from the JU 87; I had hit him heavily. The Stuka went into a steep dive and opening the throttle I followed hard after it. Suddenly I realised that this was a foolish thing to do, so I immediately pulled out of my dive and began to take evasive action. The last I saw of the JU 87 it was still diving toward the murky water of the English Channel."

152 Squadron. Sgt. R. Wolton, with P/O Holmes and P/O Deanesly shot down a Dornier 17 on July 25th. Whilst at Warmwell Sgt. Wolton led a charmed life, he survived being shot down into the Channel and being thrown from his aircraft on another occasion.
Cooke/Marsh

Sgt R W Wolton, 152 Squadron, 1940

10

Roger Malengreau escaped from his native Belgium via France to the U.K., arriving in Liverpool on 7 July, after his army co-operation squadron had been devastated and put out of action by the Luftwaffe. On 19 July 1940 he was commissioned in the RAF and after a spell at 7 OTU (Operational Training Unit) he was posted to 87 Squadron at Exeter on 12 August.

Like so many pilots from abroad, his command of English was limited. Nevertheless, he was soon in action, flying his first operational sortie the day after his arrival. A few days later he was in action again but in the melee became detached from the remainder of the squadron and was lost in a seemingly vacant sky. Finding two Spitfires apparently descending as though they were approaching an airfield, he tagged onto the rear and followed them into Warmwell.

"I had just escaped from Belgium and had no experience as a fighter except for a few hours at O.T.U. I could barely understand English when I was commissioned in the RAF. Luckily I was greatly helped by my marvellous British friends in the squadron.

"On my second mission on 17 August I fired at a German bomber but was soon separated from the rest of the squadron and found myself alone in the sky. Having no maps I turned around until I saw two Spitfires going to land and I followed them and found myself at Warmwell.

"I was immediately surrounded by the crew, armourers and mechanics who asked me if I had any luck and where I was coming from. My broken English aroused suspicion and I was told to stay put in the cockpit. I presume they thought I might be a German as some Hurricanes left in France had apparently been used by the enemy.

"Anyhow after a while an officer arrived and I managed to explain that I belonged to 87 and had lost my way. It took quite a time to check with Group before I was re-fuelled and allowed to fly back along the coast. Everyone was by then very friendly."

P/O Roger Malengreau, 87 Squadron, Exeter

*****

In 1990 the author arranged a commemorative exhibition about RAF Warmwell at the Dorset County Museum in Dorchester, for the duration of the summer season. Roger Malengreau visited the exhibition and enquired whether he could meet me. He arrived at my place of employment to congratulate me on the content of the exhibition. Following this meeting he and I corresponded on a number of occasions and, in one letter he charmingly wrote of the museum *display "If I chased you around Dorchester it was because I was impressed by your single-handed effort at the Museum."* He also added *"Warmwell was really our sister station while I was with 87 Squadron at Exeter as her Spitfires used to provide us top cover."*

Roger Malengreau survived the war and entered the Belgian Diplomatic Service, serving as ambassador to Malaysia, Singapore and Chile. In recognition of his war service he was awarded the CBE by the British Government.

*****

The heavy defensive fighting over Warmwell at tea-time on August 25, 1940 is recalled by Sandra Stabler. Her memories are tinged with childhood bravado but tainted by sombre reality as she stood in silence and witnessed funeral processions march past her school conveying the remains of fallen servicemen to the small church of Holy Trinity, Warmwell.

"Children never view events in the same way as grown-ups and we saw no danger in watching dog-fights between planes from the airfield just up the road, and the German fighter planes. I soon discovered that if I ran to the bottom of the garden when the air-raid siren sounded, peered over the fence and looked towards the airfield I could see if there was a yellow or a red flag flying. If yellow then the fighting planes were over the English Channel but if red then the danger would be overhead, which meant the airfield was being targeted and we would make for the "dug-out" with great haste."

-oOo-

"Sunday 25th August brought about a turning point in my life in Crossways. A tea-time raid inflicted heavy bombing on the airfield (there was no time to check my flag THAT day!) We quickly made for the shelter and spent an anxious time waiting for the air raid to end. We found that the flying shrapnel and bomb blast had caused damage to our home, so that night was spent with relations who lived in a wooden building on Tadnoll Heath."

-oOo-

"My sister, brother and I went to the small village school in Warmwell and often during that summer we watched the funeral processions passing the school playground. The airmen would slow-march from the airfield to the little church in Warmwell, accompanying their dead comrades for burial in the churchyard there. The coffin would be draped with the RAF flag, with the dead pilot's cap set on top. The solemnity of the occasion must have made a great impact on us children, for we always watched in silence."

Sandra Sewell, Crossways Resident

*****

A peaceful Sunday, 25 August 1940

"We certainly knew what the war meant one Sunday in 1940. It was the afternoon of August 25th when we heard the double siren sound, so we knew that a raid was on course for the camp. Quickly, we went to the shelter in the garden. About 15 minutes later we could hear the German planes coming and also the planes taking off from the camp. It was minutes before they attacked. A few bombs dropped in Dick o' th' Banks Road but I don't think too many landed on the camp. Two bombs landed near our shelter – one about 25 yds behind it and the other not far away on the right hand side. The blast ripped out the side of the shelter and we could see plenty of daylight – the dust and noise was awful. The raid lasted about 20 minutes and then the all clear was given. My ear drums were cracked with the blast and I still have trouble today.

When we came out of the shelter after the raid we found that our house had been badly damaged and we had lost a lot of things. We also found a donkey (which I think belonged to our neighbours) with a rope around its neck, wrapped around a tree. It was OK but very shaken.

Straight after the air-raid a Mrs Wearne came and collected us three boys and took us to her house, just off Green Lane, while Mother and Father sorted things out. Almost before we had had time to have a drink we had to be moved out of her house because there was an unexploded bomb in the garden of her house.

The first night after the raid we stayed with Admiral Duff who lived at Vartrees. Within 2 days a very kind lady called Mrs Bishop, who owned the coalyard at Moreton Station, gave us 2 rooms in her house. We were very lucky."

Vic Pullen, MBE, Broadmayne Resident (Wartime Crossways Resident)

*****

Augusta Bugler lived with her parents in the family home named Weyauwega adjacent to the airfield in the village of Crossways. She attended the two Empire Air Day displays that the station staged. Prior to the outbreak of hostilities, however, the family moved to the nearby village of Owermoigne but retained their property at Crossways.

She describes the events of Sunday 25 August 1940. It was tea-time; Warmwell's personnel were taking a break when the alert was given.

"I was living with my family at Weyauwega when I attended the open day at Warmwell Aerodrome. Fortunately, we left our home and moved to Sunnybrook in Owermoigne before the war started in 1939. Crossways was then a tiny hamlet, consisting of Dick o' th' Banks Road, a shop, a garage, farmland, a few bungalows, then heathland – remote, a peaceful haven for wild birds.

My father let Weyauwega to an Army Officer stationed at Bovington Camp. After the first bombing of the Airfield, my father received a telephone call informing him that they could no longer rent Weyauwega, as the doors and windows had been blown out!

When war was declared on 3 September 1939, I joined the ARP as a messenger and was presented with the only available tin hat, which I found to be very heavy. It was always on the empty seat beside me in the car – never on my head!

Some time after my mother's death in 1940, my father thought he would like to see the bomb damage in the Weymouth and Portland areas.

Petrol was not rationed then, so off we went.

On our return, we visited my uncle and aunt who lived in a bungalow next to the garage. Suddenly, on that Sunday afternoon, the sirens screamed out a warning message. Hardly, had it died down when the roar of aircraft could be heard coming nearer and nearer. It was horrible, frightening, unreal – I knew not what to do. I imagined the ARP would be ringing me to go to Crossways and I had no way of letting them know that I was already there!

My uncle insisted that I should go down into the air raid shelter which I did, after saying I had better lock up the car. I was hardly down before the first bombs hit the countryside. Many followed gradually receding into the distance. Then came a strange silence. After a while I stood up in the shelter and said "We had better sing 'God Save the King'".

After the all-clear, I left my father, who was looking ill, to see if Weyauwega was still there. It was, plus a huge crater just outside, which was filled with water. A retired Admiral seemed to be helping, so I told the people who were gathering around to come to my home – if it was still there. I took my father to a very sympathetic Doctor and when I eventually arrived back at Sunnybrook quite a few people were there who had lost their homes. Eventually, they were less shocked and able to begin making arrangements for their futures."

Mrs Norrie Woodhall, ARP 1940/45

*****

Francis 'Dinky' Howell was a sergeant pilot on 87 Squadron and was scrambled with Sgt. Wakeling on 25 August when Warmwell was targeted by the Luftwaffe. 10 Group scrambled every available fighter to defend the airfield. Speaking of that day he commented *"I was leading a section of three aircraft, Sid Wakeling was with me one moment and gone the next. What happened to him I did not know."*

When the author met 'Dinky' Howell at his Dorchester home, he did not know where Sgt. Wakeling was buried. I explained that he had crashed near Dorchester and was buried at Holy Trinity church, Warmwell.

"I never knew that. I used to drive past the church on my way to work. I never knew he was there."

Sgt. Howell, 87 Squadron, RAF Exeter

*****

87 Squadron Hurricane drawing.
In his book 'Arise to Conquer' (published during the war) Ian Gleed described flying to Warmwell to attend the funeral of his C.O. S/L Lovell-Gregg, killed in action on 15 August 1940. Gleed, comanding 'A Flight' frequently flew P2798 LK-A and probably flew the Hurricane to the funeral at Holy Trinity, depicted in a drawing by the author.

14

Eric Westrope stepped from the train at Moreton Station to view the night sky, illuminated with falling flares, against a backdrop of a heath fire. It was his initiation to RAF Warmwell, the evening of 28 August 1940. He spent the remainder of that night in an air raid shelter.

The next day he was ordered to join the Honour Guard to accompany the funeral of Sergeant S. R. E. Wakeling of 87 Squadron which operated from RAF Exeter. Sidney Wakeling had lost his life defending Warmwell during the late afternoon raid on 25 August.

"As raw recruits, and fresh trained in slow marching I formed part of the escort to bury a Fighter Pilot at Warmwell churchyard. The only mourner present was the pilot's father.

"The coffin is lowered into the grave and a rifle salute is fired. That is the first funeral I have ever attended."

Aircraftsman Eric Westrope

*****

Although not confirmed by date the following descriptive account of an enemy aircraft crashing near Bath and a Spitfire lying nearby describes with near certainty, the death of twenty-year-old Sgt. Kenneth Holland, an Australian who, with 3 other fighters attacked a Heinkel 111 bomber during combat over Somerset on 25 September 1940. Sgt. Holland, having severely hit the Heinkel, saw flames issuing from the stricken aircraft and one of the crew bale out and his parachute deploy. Closing on the bomber (perhaps to ensure its destruction), his Spitfire was hit by return fire. One of the Heinkel's gunners fired at the speedily approaching fighter. Both aircraft crashed at Church Farm, Woolverton. Four crew members of the Heinkel were killed, two died in the crash and two others fell to their deaths, their parachutes failing to fully deploy. Only the pilot of the bomber survived the encounter. In the aftermath, local children dashed to the crash site.

"In the morning several of us village children jumped on our bikes and went to find it, hoping to get some bits to boast about at school. We were stopped from getting too close, however, by a policeman, but we did see swastikas on the wreckage. Our excitement soon died, however, when we saw the Spitfire, lying in the same field; its cockpit smashed. A man standing nearby recounted the sad event to us. "'E could've got away but came back to 'ave another look. The rear gunner got 'im." War was suddenly, horribly real. We got no bits.

The Frampton Arms at Moreton was the wartime local for airmen based at Warmwell. When the airfield was dismantled, the landlord saved mementos. Much later, it was decided to display some of them in the bar. My husband agreed to mount on wood various small parts of planes, among them a fragment of windshield and I now wonder whether this could have come from that Spitfire I saw all those years ago because I remember reading an article in a back copy of the Dorset Life magazine which explained that Spitfires from Warmwell had defended Bath. The article went on to relate the story of one Spitfire in particular, whose pilot was tragically killed because, having shot down an enemy bomber, he flew back to follow it down, to be certain of success. Sadly, the rear gunner had still been firing."

Mrs N Durigg, Wool, Dorset. 1940

Sgt. Holland's body was returned to Warmwell and was later cremated at Weymouth. (AC)

*****

Don Cooper's family had lived in the Tyneham/Kimmeridge area for generations. His sister taught in the village school at Tyneham. He knew the paths and tracks across the Purbeck cliffs from Lulworth to Swanage intimately. Excused military service because he worked on the land, he served in the Local Defence Volunteers/Home Guard, mounting guard duty along the cliff pathways. His location gave him a grandstand view of the conflict that evolved overhead throughout the summer months of the Battle of Britain.

On Friday 27 September 1940 he formed part of a patrol that saw a Messerschmitt 110 attempting to force land. The aircraft passed close to the patrol, which gave immediate pursuit as the enemy aircraft disappeared from view. Out of their sight, a short distance away, it ploughed across the ground and skidded to a halt. The patrol scrambled through a hedge to see the crew was out of their aircraft.

"It looked like they were going to set fire to the plane. Someone said to fire over their heads, so some of us fired in their direction. The crew got the message and stopped what they were doing and we went over to them and took them into custody, almost at the same time some soldiers appeared to claim the prize.

"We knew the soldiers as they were based nearby. They took the crew away, that was the last I saw of them. Some of the soldiers remained and mounted guard over the German plane."

Don Cooper

The Messerschmitt Me 110 from 8/ZG26 was crewed by Unteroffizi Schupp and rear gunner Gefreiter Nechwatal, who formed part of the fighter screen protecting bombers attacking Bristol. Reports indicate that one or both of the crew were wounded, whether this was during fighter action or when the machine force-landed is unclear. Their wounds could not have been serious, however, as Don Cooper did not comment on the state of the crew when interviewed. The soldiers were from the 4th Battalion. East Yorkshire Regiment, who detained the prisoners at their H.Q. In the Dorset Constabulary's Chief Constable's report of that day, it was noted that the machine was marked as '3U + DS' and was damaged. The incident was timed at 11:35 hrs.

-oOo-

At approximately the same time as Don Cooper's Home Guard section was capturing the crew of Messerschmitt Me 110 3U + DS, Charlie Upshaw was hunting rabbits in the fields adjacent to the road from Cheselbourne to Piddletrenthide, near Kingcombe. He was taking little or no notice of the action being fought out above, as his concentration lay totally with the rabbit he had just caught. As he bent over to pick it up: *"There was suddenly a big thud behind me. I turned around to see a man lying in the grass just a few feet from where I was standing. He was totally naked, all his clothes were gone. Bits and pieces of metal started raining down and as I went to him some of his personal possessions began to flutter down nearby. If I remember rightly t'was his wallet, watch and some other things, which I quickly grabbed up and took home with me, but with all the bits falling all around I thought it best to get out of the field.*

"When the police arrived I told them what happened and what I'd found." (Strangely, the police did not take the man's possessions but left them with Charlie Upshaw.)

"Later when the RAF arrived I went back to where it happened, but the wreckage lay there for some while until the RAF came back and collected up what was on the surface.

I helped to move the bits toward the gate where they remained until collected."

One day a man came to the house and said he was a relative of the pilot, so I gave him the possessions that I had found. I think he was a cousin of the pilot."

Charlie Upshaw, Cheselbourne

The incident that Charlie Upshaw described was the collision between Pilot Officer R. Miller of 609 Squadron and a Messerschmitt Me 110 of 9/ZG26 3U + FT. The collision caused Miller's Spitfire X4107 to explode and disintegrate. The enemy aircraft crashed at Doles Ash, a couple of miles away. Gefreiter Jackstedt managed to bale out of the blazing aircraft but Gefreiter Lidtka died in the wreckage and was later buried under a hedge near where the burnt-out Messerschmitt lay. Fragments from both aircraft were scattered over a wide area, especially spent cartridge cases, which rained down as the two aircraft fired at each other.

At that time, Charlie and Don did not know each other. Later, however, Don Cooper and his sister, Ida, moved to Cheselbourne and Don and Charlie became good friends, often enjoying a glass at the village pub, the Rivers Arms.

*****

Stories relating the exploits of P/O Pooch are legion, the canine mascot of 152 Squadron is reputed to have sired half of the dog population of Dorset! His descendants still roam the county today. In the annals of the squadron's history Pooch was held with the fondest regard and highest esteem.

"No matter what anyone says, Pooch was THE daddy of them all who apparently belonged to a Pilot Officer, Graham Cox. When 152 Squadron moved out East, Pooch remained in the charge of a pilot recovering from a bad crash. I last saw the dog in June

Pilot Officer POOCH (left) 152 Squadron's mascot and Acting Station Officer Jill. Cooke.

1941 when I left for Biggin. In 1945 I was back at Biggin Hill and found that Pooch resided in the local village of Leaves Green, and I went to see him. I walked up the path and through a door to the back garden from whence came children's voices. When I got through the door and turned, I was greeted by a menacing bull terrier intent on looking after the children. I called out with a well remembered phrase and the recognition was immediate. He put me flat on my back and just about licked the skin from my face. A wonderful old fellow."

W L H Johnson, Sgt. Pilot, 152 Squadron

*****

At the height of the Battle of Britain squadron personnel were assisted by men drafted in from the Central Gunnery School and 10 Bombing & Gunnery School. They rearmed and serviced the Spitfires and Hurricanes of all the squadrons which operated from the aerodrome during those hectic summer weeks. Here a draftee flight mechanic attached to 152 Squadron describes the events of September 27th 1940:

"As the weeks went by, the threat of an airborne invasion became a possibility, so that out at the dispersal we had rifles and ammunition. Some did a ground gunners' course and I was trained on the Lewis gun. One day during a 'Take Cover' alert I dived into our slit trench as a heck of a battle was taking place. Two machines collided in mid-air, others were shot down and I remember seeing three parachutes coming down. Minutes later Spits and Hurricanes started landing for re-fuelling and re-arming and everyone was busy in spite of Jerry."

LAC Ronald Clish, Central Gunnery School, 152 Squadron, 1940

*****

The Airmen's Club

Group Captain George Howard, Station Commander, RAF Warmwell, 1940/41, has a reputation as being an over-strict disciplinarian, often at loggerheads with the commanding officers of the fighter squadrons. It has to be understood that Warmwell was first and foremost a bombing and gunnery training station responsible for the provision of future airgunners and bomber crews. In many respects the fighters were an inconvenience to the smooth running of the station – moreover, the somewhat relaxed discipline of squadron life did not mirror the spit and polish of the training regime. However, it was Howard's opinion that the NAAFI could not cope with the vast numbers of men and women on the station. In an effort to provide somewhere for the personnel to relax when off duty he approached Lady Ellenborough, within a matter of days the Airmen's Club was born.

Jeanette Newcombe describes how the club was formed:

"I first met Lady Ellenborough in 1935 and we became family friends. She gathered together all the people she knew and started up the club after being approached by G/C Howard.

We had two shifts, one for the morning and one in the evening. I was cook for the morning one. We did egg and chips, sausages, sandwiches and so on. Although the food was rationed Lady Ellenborough, through her many friends, was able to get masses of eggs from a local farm and all the supplies she required. A girl also drove a mobile canteen which Mrs Redfern presented to the camp. The pilots who were at readiness could not leave their aircraft, so the canteen was driven to them.

Mrs Redfern often rode around the dispersal on a horse accompanying the canteen."

Jeanette Newcombe, Airmen's Club 1940/41

G/C Howard was under considerable pressure from both the Air Ministry and governing body of the NAAFI to have the Club disbanded. He resisted all approaches, however, and it took the intervention of the Luftwaffe to achieve what the Air Ministry could not. The Club was forced to close shortly after the disastrous raid of 1 April 1941.

*****

The attrition rate of pilots during the Battle of Britain was great. Fresh pilots were drafted to fill the ranks, many would not survive their first engagements; however even experienced pilots were lost. Sgt. A W Kearsey joined 152 Squadron in August. He became friends with Pilot Officer Harold Akroyd who died on October 7th. His Spitfire crashed at Wynford Eagle and not, as is reported in many books, near Blandford Forum.

"Before joining 152 Squadron I served at Warmwell with No. 10 Bombing & Gunnery School and had almost 400 hours in my log book however I had had no experience of combat. P/O Akroyd and I became friends, as did our respective wives.

"On October 7th we were scrambled and I recorded in my flying log "ME110 & 109s, 30 JU 88s intercepted. P/O Akroyd did not return from the combat, which was great indeed – it was spread over a large area. He was very badly burnt and taken to Dorchester hospital where he died.

"As I knew him quite well I was asked if I would go and see his wife. It was a duty I found distressing; it was very sad. He had recently been promoted from sergeant to pilot officer, however at the time of his death was still wearing his sergeant's uniform. Later my

Pilot Officer A W Kearsey, 152 Squadron, 1940.
Cooke.

wife met his wife in Dorchester, She was taking his unworn uniform back to the tailor who made it, in the hope that he would buy it back."

Pilot Officer A W Kearsey, 152 Squadron, 1940

*****

The civilian population, especially those living in the southern counties, witnessed the daily dog-fights of the Battle of Britain. They were soon to be 'combatants', when the Luftwaffe diversified its tactics and began the systematic bombing campaign known as the Blitz, to destroy major towns and cities. Often the air-raid sirens were late. The first that the population would know of an action beginning was the resonant sound of racing aero-engines as overhead, numerous combat encounters were being fought out.

Joan Watts, employed as a domestic companion to Miss Hilda Tilly, was preparing vegetables in the kitchen when she heard the sound of aircraft flying very low nearby. She slipped out to the rear of the house where she had a view to the east. Vapour trails outlined against the sky traced the passage of the adversaries fighting way above her.

"It was a very calm day, blue sky with almost no cloud. I heard all these roaring and diving aeroplanes and rushed out into the back garden and saw two aeroplanes down very low, they appeared as though they were right above me. Smoke was trailing from the back of one of them. Moments after a parachute opened and I watched a fellow trailing down.

"The other aircraft, which I was later told was a German, circled round and round the man on his parachute. As I watched it drifted out of sight, whilst above me other planes were still buzzing about.

"Later I was told an aircraft crashed near West Stafford and that the pilot had landed nearby. We were never told anything in those days, rumours were plenty, someone actually said that the man on the parachute was being shot at by the other aeroplane but I cannot confirm if this was true. There were so many stories flying about."

Joan Watts, The Chestnuts, Dorchester

Regrettably, although Joan vividly recalls the action, she was unable to date the encounter. It is, therefore, impossible to confirm the actual occasion to which she is referring but it is probable that she is talking of the fighting of either 25 August or 7 October. On both occasions, fighters fell near Dorchester. Without information about the unit the pilot and aircraft came from, it will have to remain speculative but Joan is sceptical of the latter date as the weather that day was bright and clear and very warm.

*****

Dennis Fox-Male was a qualified solicitor prior to joining the RAF. He was posted to 152 Squadron in September 1940. On October 10th he fought in an engagement in which 56 Squadron from Boscombe Down and 238 Squadron Middle Wallop each lost an aircraft.

"The squadron was scrambled on an 'X Raid' patrol. B Flight was led by F/O Marrs. I was flying on his port side leading Sgt. Szlagowski.

About noon we were flying around some cumulus cloud in close formation when suddenly an Me109 came past us on the port side, about fifty yards away. We were flying in opposite directions. It was too late to do anything but there was probably a second 109 with him but I didn't see him. Unknown to me, Szlagowski turned sharply and went into a spin. I did not know that. The next thing was that I had some bullets from behind into the cockpit, wings and engine. Glycol streamed out of the tank ahead. The formation broke and scattered and I started to bale out but the glycol leak stopped, I got back into my seat and flew back to Warmwell. One of the bullets had just gone over my head and through the top of the glycol tank."

Pilot Officer Dennis Fox-Male, 152 Squadron, 1940

*****

The extreme youth of those both on the ground and in the air is characterised by Ronald Clish.

"When 152 and 56 Squadrons arrived things started buzzing. During a scramble it was nothing unusual to see 9 or 12 Spitfires and 9 Hurricanes taking off 3 abreast, one line behind another. The roar of engines was deafening in the hangar.

"The pilots were a grand lot of lads, some of the Sgt. Pilots were like myself, only 20 or 21 years old. Straight from college or grammar school to Flying Training Units and on to a fighter squadron. Outwardly they were a happy-go-lucky, couldn't care less lot."

LAC Ronald Clish, Central Gunnery School, 152 Squadron, 1940

*****

During the night of 6 November 1940 a Heinkel He 111 force landed on the rock shelf at West Bay. It is believed that the machine, from KGr 100 (Kampfgruppe 100) based at Vannes, was acting in a pathfinder role and had suffered a compass failure. Disorientated, it passed over the Bristol Channel, perhaps leading the pilot to believe he was over France. It was a fair feat of flying, landing in darkness on a narrow pebble beach and skidding off onto the rock shelf. He finally came to rest beneath a large outcrop known locally as Table Rock.

Over the next few days, most of the population of Bridport turned out to view the bomber. For some it was intimidating.

"It lay there, black and menacing, the sea washing around it."

Amy Dimmick, Bridport Resident

The author, who was born and lived in Bridport until 1960, also has recollections of this aircraft.

In 1958 one of the Heinkel's engines still remained buried in the pebble and shingle beach mid-way between West Bay and Eype, where it must have been wrenched off the machine as it skidded along the beach and across the rock shelf.

With three schoolboy pals we dragged a go-cart belong to Pat Pearce down to West Bay and along the beach. It was hard going, hauling the go-cart over the shingle. Our goal was to dig up the engine and triumphantly bring it home!

After a day's hard work, we achieved little and never succeeded in our quest, because for every spade full of shingle we moved, two seemed to take its place. The beach won the contest and we finally gave up and, dejectedly, trudged home.

The engine, at this time, was in a good state of preservation and appeared undamaged or corroded by the sea. Someone had removed one of the covers exposing the rocker arms and valve springs but the oil remaining in the cylinder head was black, smelt strongly and had not been diluted with sea water.

By 1970, the engine had corroded beyond recognition. Someone had retrieved part of it and thrown one of the pistons and connecting rod, with part of the cylinder block attached to it, on to the small beach, which once formed part of the harbour area. This was the last vestige of history relating to this incident.

*****

1941

The Widge and the Ibsley Wing 1941

As the RAF went on a limited offensive basis in the spring of 1941, various squadrons were formed into operational Wings, which were located on a single airfield. Normally a Wing would comprise of three squadrons. With the formation of the 2nd Tactical Air Force later in the war, the Wings were issued with a number, as opposed to the airfield location, in preparation for the forthcoming invasion of Europe.

RAF Ibsley was opened as a satellite to Middle Wallop in February 1941. By April, 32 Squadron had vacated the station and 118 Squadron arrived, to be joined by 501 Squadron in August and 234 Squadron in November. S/L Ian 'Widge' Gleed, then commanding 87 Squadron, was promoted to Wing Commander Flying, Middle Wallop. An inspired choice, he galvanized the three squadrons into the Middle Wallop Wing. It was more popularly known as the Ibsley Wing, after its operational base.

The Wing frequently worked with Warmwell's fighter-bomber squadrons to provide operational fighter cover. Commanding one of these squadrons was S/L Christopher 'Bunny' Currant, DFC & Bar, a veteran of the Battle of France and the Battle of Britain. He would lead 501 Squadron.

Christopher Currant regarded Wing Commander Gleed as an exceptional pilot - a charismatic and emphatic leader. Both Gleed and Currant joined the RAF in 1937 and served together flying Gloster Gauntlets in 46 Squadron at Kenley. The following is Christopher Currant's account of a night flight he and Gleed made over London. It demonstrates their youthful exuberance and skill in the air, skill that they both would need in the war that was all too soon to become a reality.

"In our early days at RAF Kenley we did something which I wonder if anyone else has ever done, either before or since. It was 1937. We were night flying. Widge took off first along the flare path. I followed and by pre-arrangement joined up with him above Kenley at 10,000 feet. It was a glorious bright brilliant moonlit night in mid-summer.

"We flew over London in tight formation – about twelve feet apart. The air was still and smooth as silk. We found Piccadilly Circus clearly visible and easily picked out by reference to the Thames, Westminster Bridge and the Houses of Parliament, all so clear in the full moon.

"We then dived down and pulled up and over in a complete loop slap over Piccy Circus. Then we returned to Kenley and landed singly and excitedly shared our thrill and enthusiasm over the trip. We never told anyone. We didn't dare, or we might have been Court Marshalled. Such is youth! Happy, happy days."

A short time later, in daylight, Currant and Gleed had a practice dog-fight, a frenetic combat against each other where neither would yield.

"I once had a dog-fight with him and for the first and only time ever, was air-sick, my head drooped over the edge of the open cock-pit. I never let on to him. No way.

"Later, on Hurricanes, I did many, many hours of formation aerobatics in a tight Vic of three. Heavenly moments I'll never forget. I so loved it all. Widge Gleed and I were great buddies. A great little guy was Widge."

S/L Currant played a cameo role as himself in the Leslie Howard/David Niven film "The First of the Few" which chronicled the story of the design of the Spitfire. Much of the filming was shot at Ibsley, with other scenes filmed at Christchurch and, briefly, Warmwell. Leslie Howard's brother, Arthur, was the Station Adjutant and their cousin, George Howard, was Warmwell's Commanding officer.

-oOo-

Spitfire Embrace

The Spitfire was not the easiest aircraft to taxi. Its high, long nose required the pilot to constantly swing the machine from left to right to gain forward vision when taxiing. Due to a spate of accidents, Wing Commander Gleed summoned the squadron commanding officers of the Ibsley Wing to his office and gave them a lecture regarding the apparent lack of caution exercised by pilots. Each returned to his squadron and 'roasted' the assembled gathering. Later that day S'/L Currant led 501 Squadron to Warmwell where, during taxiing to a halt, he almost collided nose to nose with another machine from the squadron.

"Two Spitfires kissing in public – bloody embarrassing as I had that morning had all the pilots together at Ibsley and threatened them with hell itself if anyone dare be so stupid as to have a taxiing accident.

"Ye Gods – how the mighty have fallen. When we got back to Ibsley I called them all together again and said "There see … that's what happens to the stupid clot who lets his attention wander for just a moment."

Squadron Leader Christopher Currant, 501 Squadron, RAF Ibsley

In 1942 Christopher Currant assumed command of the Ibsley Wing when W/C Gleed was posted to Fighter Command H.Q. as Wing Commander Tactics. In July 1943 Wing Commander Currant was deservedly awarded the D.S.O. for his leadership and service with 501 Squadron. He retired from the RAF in 1959.

On 1 January 1943 W/C 'Widge' Gleed was posted to the Middle East. He lost his life on 16 April of that year when he was shot down in combat over the Tunisian coast and is buried in the Military Cemetery at Enfidaville.

*****

Warmwell would endure many raids throughout its operational career; the extremely well executed attack of 1 April 1941 took the station by total surprise. It was the worst raid the airfield would experience. There were ten fatalities and numerous wounded – many had narrow escapes. Kath O'Brien owed her life to an unknown soldier.

"On 1 April 1941 I was walking from the Airmen's Mess, where I was a cook, to the

WAAF's Mess when I saw 3 planes coming in, as I thought, to land. As they dived low I waved thinking they were our boys, then, within seconds, they started machine gunning and I saw the bombs falling from the planes. I was dragged to the ground by a soldier and then orders came over the tannoy to get to the shelters as quickly as possible. It was then that we learned that nine or ten had been killed in the raid.

A few days later the Duke of Kent was visiting the Airfield and the kitchen staff were all in the dining room looking spic and span, awaiting his arrival. Suddenly, there was a terrific noise, dinners went flying and the cooks dived for cover under tables expecting more machine gunning. There was a queue of people outside wondering what on earth was going on in the dining room. It transpired that we had all run for cover from a step ladder falling down along the side of the corrugated wall but after the raid a few days earlier everyone's nerves were on edge. You can imagine the panic of cleaning up before the Duke arrived and when he did appear we were all smiles as though nothing had happened."

Kathleen (nee O'Brien) Peters, WAAF, Australia

*****

The raid of 1 April 1941, and another incident, are recalled by Dick Tizzard, who was living in Crossways during the war.

"I remember the heavy attack on the airfield on 1 April 1941. We were up at the camp delivering a load of spuds, when I seen these three aircraft coming in from down by the railway line. I think about a dozen people were killed and I remember the Spitfires going off to chase the Jerries, but by then they were well away from here."

-oOo-

"I was out one day near Knighton Woods in a lorry with a load of feed for the cattle – 'twas quite foggy. All of a sudden, this twin engined aircraft come down across the field and starts shooting at me – he was so low I could see the pilot and the German markings. I guess he was looking for the airfield but couldn't find it in the poor visibility. I'm pretty sure it was a Messerschmitt 110 fighter-bomber.

Anyhow, I dived between the lorry and the hedge, and pulled a load of hay down on top of me – the bugger couldn't get me there – but he did kill a whole load of sheep in the next field."

Dick Tizzard, Crossways Resident

*****

During 1940/41 Warmwell had a thriving amateur dramatic society led by F/L Howard. Later, when ENSA shows to entertain service personnel were travelling the country, Warmwell welcomed many theatrical and film stars through its gates. There were also activities devised amongst the personnel, "liberty buses" to and from the camp to local towns and, of course, romance.

"We had entertainment on the camp: dances, housey-housey (bingo) and also shows. My (future) husband had the pleasure of picking up Anna Neagle from the railway station.

There were two liberty coaches to Weymouth every night where we all queued for the pictures (cinema). The coaches returned at 10.30 p.m. for the WAAFs to go to Moreton

House and 11 p.m. for those living on the base. Another WAAF and myself used to cycle across the heath to Bovington to the pictures.

I met my future husband at Warmwell. He was an MT driver attached to 266 Squadron, who were flying Typhoons. Their 'planes were based right on the other side of the airfield under the trees, so personnel had a long way to travel to the cookhouse. 266 Squadron were at Warmwell for approximately four months, before moving to Exeter."

Joan Laing (nee Gillett), WAAF, MT Section

*****

A WAAF arrives at Warmwell

"About the middle of October 1941 I was posted to RAF Warmwell. On being met at Moreton railway station by a WAAF corporal, I was taken to Moreton House which was one of the WAAF billets, for a meal and to stay the night.

"The next morning I reported to the WAAF Orderly Room, which was in a cottage called Var Trees. After a tour of the camp, I was taken by transport to another billet quite a distance from the camp. It was a lovely country house called Conygar situated just outside of Broadmayne.

"It was decided that I would be a waitress in the officers' mess. After a spell I was told to report to Stafford House, West Stafford. This was the main mess and quarters of the aircrew and officers of the station headquarters. An RAF Flight Sergeant was in charge of the mess and batmen and WAAF Flight Sergeant in charge of the cooks and waitresses."

Grace Curtis (nee Stent), WAAF

*****

1942/43

Alex Simpson was a flight mechanic on 175 Squadron during the summer of 1942. He was responsible for the engine of the aircraft he was allotted and acted as a spare mechanic. Consequently he worked on all the machines of B Flight.

"One morning while the Flight was busy on routine daily inspections, there was a rattle of machine gun fire and everyone dived for cover (believing the airfield was under attack). When nothing followed we all started to move around again to discover what had happened. It seemed that an armourer had just loaded all his guns (and was stood in front of the Hurricane's armed wing), when an electrician who was working alongside him said quite innocently "What would happen if you pressed the button now". Before the armourer could reply, the guns went off! Unfortunately a rigger doing his daily cockpit check only heard the words "Press the button" which he did and nearly blew the armourer's head off. He must have been one of the luckiest lads about at that time, an inch or two either way would have knocked his head off"

LAC Alex Simpson Fitter IIE 'B Flight' 175 Squadron, 1942

*****

Warmwell was responsible for the supply of a number of units in and around the county, including the air-sea rescue units and the secret radar site at Worth Matravers. Bill

175 Squadron. It is early morning, the men have just carried out the daily inspection on this Hurricane prior to it participating in an offensive operation. Alex Simpson (first left, back row) was minutes away from learning that he had been posted out of the squadron.
Cooke/Simpson

Marks, a ground defence gunner, transferred to Warmwell from Worth Matravers and experienced, as did many others, the fragrance of Knighton Woods.

"I was posted to Warmwell from Worth Matravers where I had been a Ground Gunner. My first impression of RAF Warmwell was the lovely smell of the pine trees and the beautiful Dorset countryside. All personnel were issued with a bicycle, as it was such a large area to cover between cook-house, Orderly Room, Cinema, other important buildings and one's place of work. Also, when anything went wrong with the bicycle, you took it to a WAAF Section, who maintained them. Our billets were in the middle of the woods, which could not be seen from air.

I had a nice job at Warmwell, mainly working between the Sports Ground, as Groundsman, and assisting the camp cinema operator."

LAC Bill Marks, RAF Warmwell

*****

During the summer of 1942 the 307th Fighter Squadron 31st Fighter Group USAAF came to Warmwell to attend 10 Group Armament Practice Camp. Alex Simpson, a native of Scotland, recalled an incident experienced by the Squadron and a meeting with one of the pilots who had previously force landed in Scotland.

Lt. William 'Whiskey' Whisonet 307th Fighter Squadron 31st Fighter Group USAAF flew to Warmwell with his unit for armament practice from 19th-27th July 1942. Whisonet would claim the destruction of a FW 190 fighter over Dieppe on August 19th.
Cooke/Turk

"I only had casual meetings with the Yanks. They came around the flights on occasions and picked our brains. On one occasion an engine cowl had blown off one of their Spitfires and they were searching all over the airfield for it."

-oOo-

The following incident is legendary in 307th Fighter Squadron. The pilot in question, Lt. Whisonant, had to be almost carried from the whisky factory to the transport sent to collect him. Thereafter, he was known as "Whisky" Whisonant.

"On another occasion I had a chat with one of the pilots in a Weymouth tea-room. He had heard my Scottish tongue and he wanted to let me know how much he enjoyed Scottish hospitality. On a routine training flight he had crash-landed near, of all places, the Haig Whisky factory in Fife!"

LAC Alex Simpson, Fitter IIE, 'B Flight', 175 Squadron, 1942

*****

Dr. William Turk was the medical officer of the 307th Fighter Squadron, 31st Fighter Group, 8th Air Force.

The 31st Fighter Group was comprised of three squadrons; 307th, 308th and 309th. Shortly after the squadrons had completed their conversion course to fly Spitfires, each squadron was dispatched to an armament practice camp. The 307th was sent to the 10 Group APC at Warmwell, where the squadron would encounter life on an active station. They also experienced initial distress when a pilot from 175 Squadron, whom they had befriended, failed to return from an operational sortie.

F/O 'Hank' Hannigan of 175 Squadron was a likeable, devil-may-care, Irishman who played the guitar and sang cowboy songs. Perhaps, because of his music, he helped remind the Americans of home. Hank Hannigan was lost on a shipping strike. Dr Turk remembers:

"I remember the Hurricanes. They mainly went on strafing missions. One of the pilots was an Irishman called Hank, very comical; tall slender, with a handlebar moustache. He enjoyed sticking his head and long neck above a window sill, popping his eyes and putting on a big grin. It was a funny sight."

"One day when the Hurricanes returned someone said "Ole Hank bought it." The place was never the same for us."

"The British had a different attitude about the loss of a comrade. They went about business as usual while the Americans moped around for several days."

Dr Bill Turk, M.O. 307th Fighter Squadron, 31st Fighter Group

F/O Hannigan's Hurri-bomber was hit by AA fire from a flak ship during a shipping strike on 30 July 1942. He was fairly low down when hit and had no opportunity to bale out. His squadron colleagues on the mission believed that he was probably killed instantaneously or was unconscious before his aircraft hit the sea as he made no attempt to control the machine. His Hurricane just rolled over and plunged immediately beneath the waves.

He has no known grave.

*****

The Dieppe operation was shrouded in clandestine secrecy. At Warmwell, 175 Squadron received orders to move forward to RAF Ford on 17 August 1942. The Officers' Mess became a hive of early morning activity as those preparing to leave packed their kit amid a vale of silence.

The adjutant recorded in the Station Form 540 (Warmwell's Station Diary) that the squadron had moved to Ford and that no other information was available to date.

The Officers' Mess was a close knit community but standards and protocol remained, although the mess staff were, in the main, as young as the men about to fly out to who knew what. Ida Pitfield often spoke with Pilot Officer McLaren and she recalls that morning, as she went about her duties:

"They left after breakfast, they were wearing revolvers (unusual), so I asked "Where are you going?" Mac held up his suitcase and said "Shh-shh", so we knew it was hush-hush. The news came about Dieppe and they eventually returned."

Ida Pitfield, Officers' Mess

Pilot Officer McLaren participated in the final sortie that 175 flew on 19 August. Led by Squadron Leader Pennington-Legh, eight Hurribombers left Ford at 12:50 hours to attack gun positions on the western headland overlooking the town and beaches of Dieppe. So much of the target area was shrouded in smoke and flame that not all of their objectives were successfully hit. All the aircraft returned safely to Ford.

*****

Space and accommodation were always at a premium. To the north of the railway line on the road to Woodsford, were a number of military buildings surviving from World War One. It was here, below the level crossing gates that the motor transport section was based, including crash crew and ambulance sections.

MT Section at RAF Warmwell, 1942.
Photo: Mrs. J. Laing

Joan Gillett had completed her driving course at Weeton (near Blackpool) and was posted to the MT Section, in September 1942.

"We were billeted at Moreton House and also Lewell Mill, but for personal transport most of us were issued with bikes because the airfield was so scattered. We all wore battledress in the MT Section. Eventually, the section moved on to the main 'drome which was much better.

We used to do night duty at the MT Section and also shifts at Flying Control. Our job there was to drive the airmen on to the airfield to light the lamps on the plane park. In the morning, at early light, I had to drive them back to put them out. We used to go picking mushrooms in the early hours and bring them back to flying control and cook them for breakfast. I ate so many over the weeks, that I ended up with a rash and had to drive around with white cream on my face! Whilst on night duty we had to cook our own meals which the cookhouse provided us with.

Other MT duties also consisted of driving airmen to the decoy site at Winfrith and to RAF Chickerell."

Joan Laing (nee Gillett), WAAF, MT Section

*****

To be "Off Camp" without the correct passes was a serious matter and an airman had to ensure he was back at camp well before work began, otherwise he would have a definite appointment with the Warrant Officer Discipline. For Bill Marks a 'chain of events' almost led to such an appointment.

"On 5 September 1942 I was married while still serving at RAF Warmwell, but in the months leading up to our wedding, and when not on duty, I would often cycle to my future wife's home at Eastington Farm, Worth Matravers. Occasionally, I would stay with her family before cycling back early the next morning to avoid being caught off camp. One morning, on my return journey the chain came off my bicycle and I really thought I would be for it! In desperation, I called at the first house I came to and, as luck would have it, another airman lived there who had a married man's sleeping out pass. He very kindly lent me his bike and agreed to repair mine during the day so that when I passed his house again that night I could return his and collect mine. This we did and he got me out of a very difficult situation!"

LAC Bill Marks, Warmwell 1942

*****

Warmwell's flying field was often waterlogged. In 1942/43 the heavy Typhoon fighter-bombers of 266 and 257 Squadron had to be dispersed to RAF Ibsley for operations. Meanwhile, the Whirlwinds of 263 Squadron were able to cope with the adverse conditions owing to their wide tracked undercarriage and twin engine configuration. Vic Oliver recalls the day when flight commander F/L Blackshaw stalled his machine.

"The area around the dispersal sometimes looked like a mud pond. On this particular day as the squadron taxied across the field, F/L Blackshaw, for some reason seemed slow to move off. Most of his flight were already at the far end of the field and were beginning to turn into the wind prior to making their take-off runs.

He finally moved off and was quite some way along the track when an engine cut out. We grabbed the trolley accumulator and began to slip and slide our way, dragging the heavy trolley acc. behind us. It was hard going. Blackshaw was standing in his cockpit yelling at us to "Get a move on" but it was very difficult to get a foothold.

He was red faced and fuming when we finally reached him and becoming very flustered, but we restarted the Whirlwind and he was able to take off and catch up with the squadron which had been circling over the airfield."

Vic Oliver, Engine Fitter, 263 Squadron

Returning to base after dusk, F/L Blackshaw, low on fuel after an offensive operation, attempted to reach RAF Exeter and was almost in sight of the airfield when his engine cut out and he was killed whilst attempting to make a forced landing on 16 May 1943. His body was returned to RAF Warmwell and buried with full military honours at Holy Trinity, Warmwell.

*****

Invariably, there can be more than one report of how an individual died. The author has a second account, which relates that F/L Blackshaw baled out just before his aircraft crashed. In many respects, the two reports are very similar with only slight differences. The passage of time probably means that neither of the reports will be totally confirmed.

Ida Pitfield worked in the Officers' Mess when it was located on the airfield and later when it was transferred to West Stafford House, the scene of many riotous parties. F/L

Blackshaw was obviously a popular officer, as his death sent a shock wave through the mess staff, some of whom were in tears after his funeral.

"I remember how upset everyone was and how his mother had a talk with one of the waitresses after the service. I know he has a tombstone at Warmwell - I think he was cremated."

Ida Pitfield, Officers' Mess, Warmwell

*****

Squadron Leader Geoff Warnes

Geoff Warnes was, arguably, the best C.O. 263 Squadron had during its Warmwell tenure. He was a brash man, with a thunderous voice when necessary who, on many occasions, 'threw away the book'. He treated those under his command with equal magnanimity, irrespective of rank. Those who served under him thought most highly of this capable and likeable commander. Warnes is believed to have been the first combat pilot in the RAF to fly wearing contact lenses.

"Geoff Warnes was without doubt in my mind the best commanding officer I served under during my service career. He could be strict when required and often was - and didn't believe in going by the book always and made it plain to his superiors frequently. If the weather was 'clamped down' to coin a phrase of the times, he would pick up the 'phone to sector command and simply state that 263 Squadron is now on stand down.

"He would then order the 'liberty wagon'. We then changed into our best blues and all proceeded to Weymouth. Perhaps to go to the cinema or for a meal etc. Later we would all meet up in the Golden Lion where we tested our capacities. Many party pieces were performed and many songs were sung or, I should say, rendered."

F/Sgt. Denis Todd, 263 Squadron

Geoff Warnes later lost his life after the squadron had moved from Warmwell and converted to flying Hawker Typhoons. He was seen to bale out over the Channel and struggle to climb into his dinghy. Another pilot jumped to assist him. Regrettably the rescue service was unable to locate either pilot and neither were seen again. The squadron mourned the loss of one of its most respected commanding officers.

*****

Whisky, 263 Squadron's Mascot

Whisky, like so many dogs adopted as mascots by squadrons, was held in high regard. Low and behold anyone who abused one of these revered animals.

"Whisky was an Irish Wolfhound and our mascot on 263 Squadron. Almost as large as a small pony, he thought the airfield was his own personal hunting ground.

"Unfortunately a local farmer had reason to complain that Whisky had ventured beyond the boundary. In fact he had been bothering his sheep and had become a nuisance. The farmer's parting remark was "If this does not stop, I will with regret have to shoot him".

"Some time later sad to say Whisky went missing, all the lads were upset, of course, wondering what had happened to him. Talking about it one day in the crew room, one lad happened to remark "Perhaps that farmer has shot him".

*"My God", Geoff Warnes said, "That's it, that's what has happened, that b****r has shot him, right I will shoot one of his bloody sheep".*

"The following weekend we had lamb in the Messes for dinner. It made a welcome change from spam or corned beef!"

F/Sgt Denis Todd, 263 Squadron

*****

24 October 1943

S/L Baker led a squadron strength (twelve aircraft) attack against the Munsterland, a German freighter. docked in the inner harbour at Cherbourg. The Ibsley Wing normally would have provided fighter cover but was grounded by bad weather. Baker, therefore, arranged for the Whirlwinds to provide their own cover, so not all the aircraft carried bombs.

The defences at Cherbourg were formidable. The Whirlwinds attacked amid a maelstrom of flak and anti-aircraft fire, from which none of the aircraft escaped without sustaining some damage. Two were lost and a further two suffered severe damage, which caused one of the latter to belly land and the second to experience an undercarriage collapse when the machine landed at Warmwell. F/L Mercer's aircraft was hit and dived in to the sea. Meanwhile, F/Sgt Gray fought to control his Whirlwind with one of this engines ablaze but was able to make a controlled force landing in a field. He evacuated his aircraft and made off, believing he had been undetected. He did not get far!

"Perhaps half to three-quarters of a mile – it's difficult to quantify. I thought I had escaped detection but this German with a pistol spied me. Speedily he was joined by about six others – they seemed to come from nowhere. They kept on bidding me to keep my hands up (what harm I could have done them I don't know) but they were not physically abusive. I was searched of course and had a sheath knife, but no gun. The idea of the sheath knife was to puncture the dinghy if it inflated at the wrong moment, not for taking on the enemy!"

Humorously, F/Sgt Gray added *"I also had a beret and a few words of French, but no opportunity to use same!"*

F/Sgt Len Gray, 263 Squadron

He remained a P.O.W. until repatriated at the end of the war.

*****

1944

Prior to the arrival of the 474th Fighter Group 9th USAF in the spring of 1944 and Warmwell becoming Station 454 Moreton, RAF personnel vacated the airfield except for a stores contingent (to maintain RAF Warmwell's satellite units) and transport section.

Joan Gillett was one of those who remained on the camp.

"I was one of the MT drivers left when the Americans came. I well remember their PX. It sold everything in the cosmetic line you could think of but we missed our cups of tea – it was all coffee!

My husband and I became engaged at Swanage. He had volunteered for the RAF Commandos, so was due to go to Germany. We were married in September 1945. He got

Joan and Theo Laing's wedding at Cerne Abbas in 1945, with the MT Section forming a Guard of Honour for the happy couple.
Photo: Mr. & Mrs. Laing

held up in Germany because of a blown up bridge and arrived home at Cerne Abbas two days late.

Our wedding photo is taken on the church steps at Cerne Abbas with the MT Section acting as guard of honour."

Joan Laing WAAF, MT Section

*****

23 May 1944

The 474th F.G. had already flown one mission that morning. At 4:30 pm it was airborne on its second sortie of the day attacking targets of opportunity in the Rouen area. A railroad bridge was attacked but not destroyed and Lt. Knox turned back to make another attack. His voice was heard on the R/T "I'm going back for a second pass."

He did not return from the attack. Within the Group this statement became to be considered to be the classic last words. During the operation, Lts. Roddick, Patterson and Chickering shot up two locomotives. The firepower of the P.38 was awesome.

"The four fifty-calibre machine guns and one twenty millimetre cannon in the nose of a P.38, all weapons rapid firing, made an awesome cylinder of punch, controlled by one button on the wheel control (control column) – a punch that could roll a semi-truck and trailer onto its side. But the ammunition load, limited by space and weight, provided just twenty-nine seconds of continuous fire."

-oOo-

The 474th Fighter Group experienced their first air raid.

"Air raid here the other night. Maybe we were the target. The AA guns around the perimeter jolted us out of our beds at two in the morning. A few of us rushed outside to see what was going on. An airplane screeched across the area, low by the sound. Heard machine guns rattling, but not close. Thumps of exploding bombs south of us. All quiet after a while. Returned to bed. There across the room, was good old Red, (his best buddy. AC) snoring peacefully. He missed the whole show."

-oOo-

Almost all of the P38s flown by the Group were adorned with personal emblems painted on the nose of the respective aircraft.

"Staff Sergeant Martin Steffler has turned out to be the crew chief of my airplane. Steff is a good guy, but never has much to say. The other day, he came to me out on the line and said "Er, Bill, how about if we name our airplane 'Down & Go?' That's a Black Jack expression when a player wants the dealer to give him just one more card, face down, usually called on a count of sixteen.

"It was the first time he called me by my first name, in accordance with my instructions to him, so how could I refuse? So 'Down & Go' has become my assigned airplane name – quite a splendid coat of arms is now painted on the nose. It consists of two cards, the top one spread angled out from the other one, as though being held in the player's hand. The top card is the six of hearts, the other is the ten of spades. A circle goes round the two cards with room inside the circle for the name. I think it looks great, and so does Steff."

Lt W Chickering 429 Squadron 474th Fighter Group USAAF Warmwell

*****

D Day

Augusta Bugler, like most residents of Dorset, has vivid recollections of the night of 5/6 June 1944 as aircraft after aircraft passed overhead transporting the airborne troops to Normandy.

"I recall in June 1944, one evening at dusk, the distant noise of aircraft could be heard overhead and we could see the lights going out to sea hour after hour. All through the night we heard the roar of the planes flying over our homes.

At about midnight nightingales could be heard from the little wood opposite Sunnybrook and at intervals, pheasants too, frightened by the noise. This I shall never forget.

In the morning the newspaper announced the invasion of Normandy had taken place."

Mrs Norrie Woodhall, ARP 1940/44

*****

On June 5/6th the 474th F.G. were detailed to fly convoy escort missions covering the invasion armada as it sailed across the Channel.

Strict secrecy surrounded the briefings and those officers who had been briefed in the days prior to D Day were confined to camp and placed under military guard. Lt. Chickering flew the first mission that afternoon and witnessed the events that followed.

"We learned about it last night – yesterday afternoon to be exact. A broad map covered the briefing room wall, marked in colour with the paths of the various invading forces. Omaha and Utah were the code names of the American beaches. An army officer briefed us on the overall plan. Others laid out communications call signs. A message from Gen. Eisenhower was read to us.

"When we arrived, we knew something extraordinary was up. MPs were stationed at the door. At the end of the briefing the 474th Group Chaplain offered up a short prayer. First time I seen a prayer at a briefing. Our patrol later that night went uneventfully. Weather, as usual, was a problem, however – low cloud ceiling. We encountered no enemy aircraft. Flew our patrol and came home, to be replaced by other fighters. Landed at twilight."

Lt. Chickering was not detailed to fly further missions that evening. He had supper, sat about and "shot the breeze" before going to bed and spent a restless night.

"In the still-black hours of early morning today (6th June), we were awakened by the drone of airplane engines over Warmwell. Got up and went outside. Wave after wave of airplanes, red and green navigation lights on, flying south, only a couple of thousand feet above our heads. From the briefing, we knew they were C-47s towing gliders filled with infantrymen and paratroopers of the 82nd and 101st Airborne Divisions.

"Shortly after sun up, some of these airplanes started coming in to land on our field. I don't know how many did, but fifteen or twenty anyway. One came in, made a lop-sided circle and let down a clumsy approach, his left wing like an upside-down drop leaf table, six or eight feet of it half-broken and sticking up in the air. He got on the ground OK, at the end of his landing run, the outer wing section collapsed down onto the ground."

Most of the C-47s made emergency landings, incredibly still managing to fly after suffering considerable battle damage, many landed with wounded crews.

"A C-47 landed and taxied right over to the (control) tower, where a few of us were standing around. A single bullet had pierced the crew compartment and killed the pilot instantly. The co-pilot had flown it back, after the paratroopers had jumped.

"Big day around here. The edges of the airfield are littered with battered airplanes,

some British. Some of them brought back wounded crews. Our medics have been taking care of them."

Lt W Chickering 429 Fighter Squadron 474th Fighter Group USAAF

*****

Telegram: 7 December 1944 To: 1149172 Haslam
RETURN TO UNIT IMMEDIATELY STOP DETAILED FOR DRAFT STOP 17 A.P.C.
WARMWELL STOP

"When ever I smell the scent of pine trees my memory immediately returns to Warmwell. When on early morning duty I would walk along the track behind the revetments, the ground was wet with dew and as the sun rose the smell of pine trees drifted on the breeze."

-oOo-

A Date with Eleanor

"Eleanor was my girlfriend. We went for a night out and the only place that boasted some resemblance of a restaurant was on the pier at Weymouth – we actually got table cloth and candle! I ordered a sumptuous meal of pheasant and pigeon pie. The pigeon was there alright in small amounts and at 5 shillings (25pence) cost a bomb. Afterwards we sat in the dark (on the pier) overlooking the bay. Finally I took Eleanor to the YWCA for a bed and I went to a Salvation Army Hostel.

"Next morning I went around for her and we cycled back to camp, arriving about 6 a.m. to report for work.

"Boy! What wild times we had with our well brought up manners."

LAC K Haslam 17 APC, 1944

*****

1945

After the 474th Fighter Group USAAF vacated the airfield in early August 1944, the RAF quickly established 14 & 17 Armament Practice Camps on the station. The APCs would service the combat Wings of 83 & 84 Groups 2nd Tactical Air Force, fighting on the Continent.

Squadrons from each Wing were dispatched to Warmwell on a rotational basis, to sharpen their gunnery and bombing skills. The sorties over the Chesil ranges were not without incident, regrettably - sometimes fatal. There was a lighter side to the attachment, however, as away from the rigours of combat flying the pilots and groundcrews could relax, let their hair down and drink the mess dry. This happened at Warmwell on more than one occasion, and tours of local breweries were high on the agenda.

Andre Lord, a French Canadian fighting with 438 RCAF squadron, summed up what most men thought when posted to the Warmwell APC. His squadron proudly answered to the sobriquet of 438 'Wildcat' Squadron, which had been adopted by the City of Montreal. Their motto: 'Going Down' reflected the hazardous nature of the operations on which the squadron was employed. They departed B78 Eindhoven on March 18th 1945 and arrived at 17 APC the next day after an overnight stopover at Manston.

"In the middle of March '45, the squadron was ordered to Warmwell (England) for a rest and an armament course – dive bombing and air to ground firing. We didn't mind the 'rest' bit, but we felt the expenditure of ordnance was a total waste of money and of our precious pub crawling time. Hell! We had been dropping bombs and shooting up ground targets for months and we considered ourselves pretty good, if I may say so. But, who are we to question the wisdom of the Brass Hats. So off we went."

F/L J.A Andre Lord 438 RCAF Squadron

*****

438 RCAF Squadron settled in after its arrival at 17 APC Warmwell to the usual business of sorties over the Chesil ranges. Sited along the Chesil Bank were a series of static targets. Aircraft would 'attack' these from the landward side of the Fleet lagoon so that the shot would fall into the water on the seaward side of the Bank. Moored in the sea, 1,000 yards off the Chesil Bank, was a bombing target raft. The aircrafts would dive on the target and release their bombs; the fall plotted by two bunkers, which were able to triangulate on the raft and measure how accurate the bombing was.

S/L Jim Hogg, 438 Squadron's C/O was not happy with the standard of bombing accuracy being achieved by his pilots. He took off in his Typhoon to assess where the problem lay, and to show them how it should be done. Sadly, he failed to return from the exercise.

Roy Oldfin describes how difficult it was to attack the raft over a glassy sea.

March 25th 1945

"Those late weeks of March were warm and bright with cloudless days and considerable haze over the water. The pilots were having trouble judging the height to release the bombs over the practice target in Lyme Bay. We were forbidden to dive from sea to land for safety reasons and, as a result we did our run and dive heading out to sea, and had no visual reference points. It was because of the haze, like flying inside a ping-pong ball, no horizon. The target was a bright white and the water was so calm that the target seemed to be suspended in mid-air.

"The pilots commenced the dive at 10,000 feet and because of the lag in the altimeter due to the rapidly diving aircraft we could not rely upon the instrument; therefore, not having any visual references, we had no idea of the correct release height, we were releasing and pulling out far too high for any reasonable accuracy. S/L Hogg was disappointed with the results and decided to go up and show us that dive-bombing under such conditions could be more accurate. It seems he held the dive too long and could not pull out in time."

F/L Ray Oldfin 438 RCAF Squadron.

S/L Hogg assumed command of the squadron on 20 January after the unit's previous commanding officer, S/L P. Wilson was killed in action on 1 January. This was a day of tremendous activity when the Luftwaffe attacked most of the allied forward fighter bases in the early hours of that frightful New Year's Day.

*****

152 Squadron Roll of Honour

Location and details of each loss to the Squadron during the Battle of Britain

P/O H Ackroyd (7 October 1940)
His Spitfire was severely damaged in combat and crashed at Shatcombe Farm, Wynford Eagle, details of which were included in the Chief Constable's report for that day. The report states that he was taken to Dorset County Hospital, where he died after being admitted with serious burns and other injuries.
(This incident has been confused with a crash at Nutmead, north of Shillingstone when P/O Staples of 609 Squadron crashed after combat. He was taken to Blandford Cottage Hospital.)

Sgt J Barker (4 September 1940)
Engaged a Dornier 17 in combat, reportedly 25 miles off the Kent coast. He baled out but was killed. He is buried in France.

P/O W Beaumont (23 September 1940)
An RAFVR Officer with a BSc degree; joined the squadron in July, scrambled on an operational sortie but the exact circumstances of his death are unknown. He is remembered on the RAF Memorial at Runnymede.

Sgt J Christie (26 September 1940)
Sgt. Christie was shot down off Swanage during an engagement with Me 109 fighters. His body was recovered from the sea and on his family's request was taken to his native Scotland for burial.

P/O R Hogg (25 August 1940)
Lost during an engagement with enemy fighters over the Channel. Sadly, his body was never recovered.

Sgt K Holland (25 September 1940)
Return fire from an He 111 which he was attacking resulted in Sgt Holland crashing at Woolverton, west of Bristol, where a memorial to him has been erected. His body was brought to RAF Warmwell and later cremated at Weymouth.

P/O J Jones (11 August 1940)
P/O Jones is buried in France, losing his life after baling out of his stricken Spitfire in mid-Channel.

P/O F Posenor (20 July 1940)
The squadron's first war casualty. A native of South Africa, he was shot down off Swanage during combat with the enemy. His body was never recovered and is recorded on the Runnymede Memorial.

Sgt Reddington (30 September 1940)
Sgt Reddington failed to return after a possible combat encounter over the Channel. He was posted as 'missing' and is commemorated on the Runnymede Memorial.

P/O D Shepley (12 August 1940)
Commemorated on the Runnymede Memorial. He was posted 'missing' after engaging some Ju 88 bombers south of the Isle of Wight. His wife and mother raised money to buy a Spitfire which was named "SHEPLEY".

Sgt E Shepperd (18 October 1940)
The only casualty of the squadron not to lose his life during combat. Circumstances revolving around Sgt Shepperd's death are shrouded in official mystery. Squadron colleagues, however, report that he was attempting to locate the airfield in exceptionally low cloud and flew into a hill at Tadnoll, Winfrith.

Sgt W Silver (25 September 1940)
His exact fate has never been determined but it was believed he was shot down by enemy action over Portsmouth, where he is buried.

P/O T Wildblood (25 August 1940)
P/O Wildblood is believed to have engaged enemy fighters over the Channel, failed to return to base and was posted as 'missing'. His name is recorded on the Runnymede Memorial.

F/L L Withall (12 August 1940)
The highest ranking war casualty of the Squadron. He failed to return after combat south of the Isle of Wight. Commemorated on the Runnymede Memorial.

The war graves at Holy Trinity Church, Warmwell.
Hann.

Roll of Honour

Fatal casualties sustained in the attack of 1 April 1941

Sergeant Pilot D E Fawcett, 152 Squadron

Flight Sergeant G M C Hipkin

Corporal G J Bleasdale

Corporal V A Tompkin

Leading Aircraftsman W H P Morey

Leading Aircraftsman A H Challen, 152 Squadron

Aircraftsman 1st Class A P Dale

Aircraftsman 1st Class K W Leonard

Aircraftswoman 2nd Class Honora Hassett

Private J D Whitney, Royal Army Service Corps

The Road to War

The aftermath to World War One, the 'war to end all wars', resulted in the retraction of Britain's armed forces, including the newly formed Royal Air Force. During the next two decades, however, various programmes of expansion would be implemented, given greater impetus as Germany once more threatened to engulf Europe in war.

Expansion of the service was relatively slow in the inter-war period, but as a number of new airfields were required to cater for the increasing number of personnel requiring gunnery and bombing training the announcement that the Air Ministry was to establish an airfield near the sleepy hamlet of Crossways in Dorset, three miles from the county town of Dorchester, caused much consternation locally and in the corridors of power at County and Rural council levels. Incensed protesters soon voiced their vociferous disapproval, given greater impetus when it was revealed that the Chesil Beach, an area of outstanding natural beauty which runs from Portland in the east to Abbotsbury in the west and offers natural protection from the sea to the lagoon on the landward side of the beach, would be the location of an armament practice range.

National and local newspapers were soon off the mark. Protesters mobilised but the demonstrations that followed did little to avert the progression of events as the Air Ministry negotiated and acquired heath and farm land from the Ilchester estate and other local landowners and farmers. The Ministry was not to be swayed by the public outcry, no matter now aggressively expressed. All too soon the main contractors moved on to the

"The Beginning" was how Sgt. Cronk described the day when he flew AVRO Tutor K3427 to Woodsford/Warmwell in July 1937.
Cooke/Cronk

site to begin construction work, aided by a number of local subcontractors, notably Watts Bros. of Dorchester, to construct an airfield measuring approximately 4200 feet in an east-west direction and, at its widest north south axis, 3600 feet.

Accommodation and domestic sites, including the officers' quarters and mess, were to be located on the eastern boundary, separated from the working area of the Station by a road known as Combe Way. Located centrally along this road was the guard room to police entry onto the business end of the complex. Erected on the fringe of the western extremity of this area was a single Type 'F' Flight Shed (drawing No. 2722-4/36), but modified from the original specification of wood and corrugated iron to a steel framed structure with an asbestos roof and side sheeting. This building immediately became known to all as "The Main Hanger", retaining this distinction until its eventual destruction in 1941 even though two new Bellman type hangars were constructed in 1940. Annexed to the rear of the hangar were the flight offices, workshops and drogue target store. Immediately behind this structure was the main store block, armoury, parachute store, garages and a 24,000 gallon aviation fuel facility.

All air traffic movements would be controlled from the watch office located to the north of the hangar, nearby which was the ambulance station and fire tender, emergency treatment room and mortuary.

Construction work was still progressing in the early spring of 1937 when the first airmen were drafted to 6 Armament Training Camp, RAF Woodsford. Hutments were as yet incomplete, and airmen marched to the site from the Royal Armoured Corps centre at Bovington Camp to finish their own accommodation and prepare the camp for its operational existence. The actual date of Woodsford's official opening is difficult to ascertain but is generally accepted as 1 May 1937. The ranges had yet to be constructed and a satellite airfield at Chickerell near Weymouth, which had been used during the First World War, enlarged to facilitate the accommodation of aircraft.

The debate about the location of the ranges still caused heated controversy as it was feared that the noise generated from gunfire and low flying aircraft would affect the breeding habits of the swans at the ancient Abbotsbury Swannery, but when operations commenced it was found that the flock took little if any notice of the aerial activity above them.

Between May and July the Station's personnel gradually increased but as yet no aircraft were allocated to the new airfield. On July 10, however, Sgt. Cronk collected Avro Tutor K3427. Arriving over the airfield he put the aircraft through some neat aerobatics before landing and taxiing to a halt in front of the hangar, where a small gathering celebrated what Cronk classed as "The Beginning".

In the weeks that followed Cronk and the other pilots collected and flew in a number of Westland Wallace II machines for conversion to target towing aircraft in the Station workshops. Meanwhile, at Lyme Regis, 37 MCU (Marine Craft Unit) was established to patrol the ranges.

To date the flying had been spasmodic, limited to the machines of the Station Flight being air tested, but the local population were soon to be aware of things to come as 206 and 220 Sqdns. arrived from their base at Bircham Newton to participate in the 1937 Annual Coastal Defence exercise. To placate the local citizens the Station Commander, Wg. Cdr. Thomas, invited them to view the airfield and the Anson aircraft of the visiting units.

Westland Wallace II. K6063 is being 'run up' prior to a flight over the Chesil ranges.
Cooke/Cronk

By late October the Station had received all but one of its target towing aircraft. The sole remaining Wallace requiring collection was an open cockpit Mk.I, which none of the pilots was enthusiastic about collecting from the armament practice camp at North Coates Fitties in Lincolnshire. It was therefore decided that straws would be drawn, and the unlucky recipient of the short straw was Sgt Cronk.

He travelled north by train but was fog-bound at North Coates until 6 November when the weather cleared slightly. Assessing that the conditions were favourable to make the return journey, he took off just after lunch. Soon he was flying through low cloud, forcing him to hedge hop over the countryside, and conditions were such that it became obvious that he must find somewhere to land before being forced to abandon the aircraft. As RAF Bicester was fairly close he decided to head in that direction. The fog was now becoming so thick, however, it was imperative he immediately found a place to land. When a sudden break in the fog revealed what appeared to be a flat field, he made a cautious approach, touched down safely and taxied across the field, gradually applying he brakes. Moments later the propeller shattered as the machine collided with a low wall which he had not seen. The tail reared up as the nose dug into the ground and the aircraft toppled over, crashing down on to its upper wing. Dazed and shaken, he released his harness and slipped to the ground, where he realised he was not alone. A wet nose and warm tongue licked his face as he looked into the dewy eyes of a beagle. All around him were dozens of dogs, each as inquisitive as the first.

Help was at hand, and eventually he returned to Woodsford, where he found that for a time he was extremely popular, everyone wanting to stand him a drink. None of the aircrew had been looking forward to flying over the ranges in an open cockpit machine, as all the unit's Mk.II aircraft had the comfort of an enclosed cockpit.

As winter deepened, a number of squadrons arrived for armament practice, the crash crew racing to the assistance of a Hawker Hind from 62 Sqdn. which overshot the boundary on November 22. A few days earlier, on 15 November, 90 Sqdn., which in June had relinquished Hawker Hinds to receive Bristol Blenheim Is, arrived at Woodsford from Bicester.

During the attachment one of the aircraft experienced a fault with its undercarriage As there was no means of communicating with the aircraft in difficulty by radio a second Blenheim was sent up to formate with it. Chalked on its fuselage were the instructions to the pilot to drop his practice bombs, use up all his fuel and land with the undercarriage retracted. Thus he probably become the first Blenheim pilot to make a forced landing, but the damage to the aircraft was minimal and was repaired in the Station workshops, allowing the machine to depart with the squadron at the end of the attachment.

Sadly this was not the last of the accidents to occur. December witnessed a further loss when a Fairey Battle of 226 Sqdn. based at Harwell, spun into the ground near the ranges.

In January 1938 the first of several Flying Training Schools began to arrive for training, and soon included 2, 6, 9 and 12 FTS. In the second week of the month 6 ATC lost its second aircraft when one of the Wallace drogue-towing machines returning from the ranges crashed into a hill at Holworth, killing both pilot and drogue operator.

Meanwhile construction work continued, and on 1 April 6 ATC became 6 Armament Training Station, operating within the confines of 25 Group. The Station staged its first Empire Air Day display during late May. Instructors from the FTSs joined the Station's pilots to perform aerial demonstrations. As the year progressed regular units of the service visited for armament practice, augmented in the summer by squadrons of the Auxiliary Air Force and occasionally machines from the Fleet Air Arm. This increase in activity brought with it an escalation in the accident rate both within the boundaries of the airfield and over the ranges, necessitating frequent long searches by the range patrol craft from Lyme Regis to locate the wreckage and recover, more often than not, the fatal consequences. At least seven further crashes occurred during the remainder of the year, including the loss of two Swordfish from the Fleet Air Arm and five training aircraft from the visiting Flying Training Schools.

On 1 July 1938 RAF Woodsford was renamed RAF Warmwell, taking its name from a nearby village to avoid confusion with the Avro factory airfield at Woodford, near Manchester. Meanwhile the training establishment continued offering live firing exercises for the benefit of visiting squadrons and schools. As each Wallace was able to stream three drogue targets before it was required to land, it could service several airgunners per target, the ammunition expended being tipped with coloured dye or ink which left traces on the canvas as the rounds passed through. On completion of streaming out, the drogue would be dropped in a field near the shore, the hits counted and relayed to Woodsford.

At the eastern end of the range two theodolite block houses were constructed 1000 yards apart, whilst moored in the bay centrally between the block houses 1000 yards off shore was a target raft. The range party triangulated on the fall of the practice bombs and

Hawker Hind K6773 came to grief when it overshot the airfield perimeter and overturned onto its upper wing section in November 1937.
Cooke/Cronk

relayed the information back to the airfield. Meanwhile to the west, at the Abbotsbury end of the range, a series of static targets was erected on the shore side of the Chesil Bank. Each pilot would dive onto his designated target and open fire, the expended rounds hitting the shingle or falling into the sea. All the ammunition was colour tipped, and as there were quite a number of targets the range party would only have to examine them between sorties or at the end of the day's activity.

The deepening crisis in Europe resulted in the mobilisation of the Observer Corps and elements of the Auxiliary Air Force, certain units returning to Warmwell. Arrivals and departures increased, including 62 Sqdn. from Cranfield, operating Blenheim Is, 217 Sqdn. from Tangmere and the Filton-based 501 Sqdn. which had been embodied into the Auxiliary Air Force. Toward the end of the year, however, 501 Sqdn. was redesignated from a day bomber unit to a Hurricane fighter squadron. Both latter squadrons were to play a further role in Warmwell's history a few months later.

Other visitors were the distinctly marked Hawker Hinds of XV Sqdn., based at Abingdon. The unit's Roman numeral fuselage identification was unique, but shortly after the squadron returned to Abingdon it exchanged its Hinds for Fairey Battles, in all probability having participated in the 1938 Empire Air Display before the conversion took place in June.

Construction work during 1939 took on a new impetus when the second and last Empire Air Day was staged as the days of peace evaporated. In June Sir Kingsley Wood announced that all civilian aircraft would be requisitioned for the duration of the war which now seem inevitable and on 24 August Britain mobilised, calling up all reservists and

Bristol Blenheims dispersed to the south of the main hangar. The unit is unconfirmed but might be one of the operational training units which flew to Warmwell for armament practice or machines from 57 Squadron.
Cooke/Foot

embodying the Auxiliary Air Force into the regular service.

Next day 10 Air Observer School was established at Warmwell, receiving an array of aircraft, including Harrows, Overstrands, Hinds, Seals, Sidestrands, Battles and some of the former unit's Wallaces, but on 1 November it was retitled 10 Bombing and Gunnery School. Six days later the Central Gunnery School was formed at Warmwell from a cadre of personnel from the former unit; pilots and aircraft being loaned from Bomber Command. Its first course commenced on 13 November, the day that Gp. Capt. G V Howard assumed command of the School from Gp. Capt. Poole. 19 days later the unit suffered its first crash when Fairey Battle K9267 force-landed at Grimstone, injuring the wireless operator.

The influx of reservists mobilised on 24 August resulted in a severe shortage of accommodation as each day men arrived at the camp gates, many without uniforms or kit. The Warrant Officer in charge of discipline went about with a permanent scowl on his face, unable to implement the dress regulations!

Late in 1939 further land was acquired to expand the western boundary to Knighton Woods while the closure of part of the highway extended the northern boundary. Work began on laying part of the perimeter track which would eventually circumvent the airfield, and to augment the single hangar and Station workshops two Bellman type hangars were constructed for the training units. However, the flying programmes continued very much as they had done throughout the previous year and would do so into the new year.

During the second week of January 1940 heavy snow falls and freezing conditions rendered the airfield unserviceable for over three weeks. The thaw again led to unserviceability as the grass flying field became waterlogged, but an improvement in the weather soon led to flying being resumed.

Spring was well under way on 22 April when Gp. Capt. Howard and his passenger were forced to abandon Master N7551 over Dorchester, the aircraft crashing near Puddletown, Dorset. Injured in the descent, the Gp. Capt. was rushed to Dorset County Hospital. A few days later he was transferred to the RAF Hospital in Torquay, where he remained until 17 May. Misfortune persisted after his return to duty; a few days later while taxiing another Master he collided with a petrol bowser!

With the large number of aircraft movements and the operations of the two training units the accident rate increased dramatically; five occurred in April alone, two in May and there was little improvement in June. 2 July proved a tragic day when Sqdn. Ldr. Ingham was killed and his passenger seriously injured when their Boulton Paul Defiant crashed on the airfield.

The Battle and Beyond

In 1936 the RAF went through a radical reorganisation programme as the new Training, Coastal, Bomber and Fighter Commands were established, the latter under the command of Air Chief Marshal Sir Hugh Dowding. Fighter Command was further subdivided into Groups – 13 Group to cover the north; 12 Group, whose responsibility it was to provide cover for the industrial Midlands, and 11 Group which would defend southern Britain from an onslaught from the continent should it eventually come. As war rapidly approached it was soon realised that 11 Group would be stretched to the limit to cover the southwest, and this resulted in the formation of a fourth defensive command – 10 Group. Moreover a weakness was identified in the defence of Portland naval base by squadrons which would be operating from the newly established sector station at Middle Wallop. This created an urgent need to make the forward airfield at Warmwell operational.

Although it was considered that in the time it would take defending squadrons to reach Portland the enemy would have hit its target and be well on the way back to the newly occupied French bases, it was not until 4 July 1940 that fighter Command considered that the construction work was advanced enough at Warmwell to sustain fighter operations and the use of the Station as a forward airfield.

10 Group's headquarters were located at Rudloe Manor, Box, Wiltshire, but the group would not become fully operational under the inspired choice of its newly-appointed commander, AVM Christopher Quintin Brand, until early August. In the meanwhile the embryo Group would share its responsibilities for operations with AVM Keith Park's 11 Group as it worked up to operational status.

Meanwhile in the aftermath of the Dunkirk evacuation Britain prepared for what appeared to be the inevitable. This seemingly invincible German war machine had blitzkreiged across Europe and was now poised on the Channel coast. At Tangmere 238 Sqdn., having reformed on 16 May, relinquished its newly-acquired Spitfires and re-equipped with Hurricane fighters, transferring to Middle Wallop on 20 June amid a flurry of activity as the sector station struggled to become operational.

For the next two weeks the squadron was to be the only operational fighter unit in the sector until 501 Sqdn. arrived from Croydon on 4 July, reinforced next day by 609 Sqdn. from Northolt, the squadron immediately detaching one of its flights to Warmwell.

Unfortunately conditions at Warmwell were far from ideal. Construction work continued and a severe shortage of accommodation resulted in the erection of tents for the squadron, a situation which it did not relish to say the least. This, and other problems, was to cause friction between the squadrons using Warmwell as a forward base and the Station Commander, Gp. Capt. Howard. Warmwell, basically a training Station, was still being run on a pre-war basis, but nevertheless 609 Sqdn. maintained one of its Flights overnight at Warmwell until 152 Sqdn. arrived from Acklington in the second week of July and became operational.

Meanwhile, to help overcome the acute accommodation problem, a number of local properties in nearby villages and those adjacent to the airfield were requisitioned for the duration of the war. At West Stafford the imposing West Stafford House was to become the Officers' Mess for station headquarters personnel and later, as the war progressed, for some of its resident squadrons. It was here in the first week of December 1942 that

152 Squadron.
UM-N UM was the squadron code letters allocated to 152 Squadron.
Cooke/Williams

accommodation was prepared for the arrival of Dr Barnes Wallis and his team to conduct initial trials to perfect Wallis's early design of the bouncing bomb.

The arrival of 609 Sqdn. on 5 July was not the first time that the squadron had visited Warmwell. Having moved to Northolt on 19 May, the unit had flown fighter cover missions over the Dunkirk evacuation, during which RAF casualties amounted to 87 pilots either dead or captured, including a number from the Squadron.

Succeeding Neville Chamberlain as Prime Minister, Winston Churchill, desperate to ensure that the French would continue fighting, made two trips to France during June. 609 Sqdn. was given the honour of escorting the Premier, moving forward to Warmwell the preceding day to rendezvous with his aircraft prior to the flight across the Channel and landing at a French airfield which retained little or no facilities.

While Churchill and his party were locked in talks with the French, the escorting pilots spent a rough night. The next day was equally fraught and no petrol was immediately available, resulting in the Premier's aircraft leaving before its escorting Spitfires were refuelled. Without access to trolley accumulators the fighters had to be started by hand-cranking the engines, thereby causing further delay.

Twenty-four hours later the squadron again escorted the Premier to France in a further futile effort, but this visit only lasted four hours. At Warmwell, elements of the Dorset Regiment, mobilized the previous August, worked to strengthen the perimeter and guard the airfield as a number of RAF personnel were drafted to form squads to defend the Station from aerial attack. Meanwhile, on heathland at Red Bridge, approximately 2 miles south of the airfield, work began on the Q site, Warmwell's decoy airfield, but today it is impossible to trace the site as it is buried beneath the rambling former Atomic Energy Establishment, Winfrith.

The month of July opened with the fatal accident which claimed the life of Sqdn. Ldr. Ingham and seriously injured his observer in the wreckage of their Boulton Paul Defiant in a horrific crash whilst returning from a weather reconnaissance over the Chesil ranges. Two days later the Station stood to attention as the Sqdn. Ldr's. ashes were scattered over the flying field. This was the day when 609 Sqdn. moved forward to the airfield and Portland harbour and its installations received the first of many violent attacks which the naval establishment would endure over the coming years.

Sgt. A W Kearsey, airborne over the harbour as he returned from the ranges, was astonished to find himself suddenly in formation with a number of Junkers Ju.87s as they peeled off to dive on HMS Foylebank. Manoeuvring his Fairey Battle into position so that his observer could engage the enemy, he joined the throng of twisting aircraft. When the man in the rear of the machine failed to fire Kearsey yelled to him over the R/T to open fire. "I can't" came the reply, "No gun!" Beating a hasty retreat, the sergeant raced across the harbour and made for base.

By 9 July the weather had deteriorated considerably but a scramble late in the afternoon resulted in three Spitfires from 609 Sqdn. engaging a formation of Ju.87s and escorting Me.110s off Portland. During the combat Flg. Off. Crook claimed a Ju.87 destroyed, but Flg. Off. Drummond-Hay failed to return from the action. Further losses over the Channel occurred on the 11th when Plt. Off. Mitchell was killed and Flt. Lt. Barran's Spitfire was seen to trail smoke as he attempted to reach the coast. Forced to bale out, he was recovered from the sea but succumbed to his injuries before the rescue vessel could reach the shore.

Meanwhile 152 Sqdn. began to move south over the two-day period of 11 and 12 July, and 10 BGS left for Dumfries. Two days later Gp. Capt. Howard assumed command of the Station as 152 Sqdn. prepared for operations, losing their first casualty, South African volunteer Plt. Off. Posener, on the 20th. Five days later the squadron avenged his loss by destroying a number of Ju.87s and a Do.17 which crashed at Fleet, near Weymouth.

Sgt. R Wolton, forming part of a three-man section led by Plt. Off. Holmes, heard Peter Devitt call "Tally Ho" over the R/T as the squadron prepared to engage. Wolton's earphones suddenly became alive with the chatter of battle. He described his first combat encounter as Holmes turned to attack a Do.17.

"The three of us, our eyes darting around the sky, made for a Dornier 17. Holmes banked and made a pass, and seconds later I followed him in. The Dornier came into my gunsight and I pressed the fire button. My Spitfire shuddered under the recoil as I watched my tracer ammunition strike home; seconds later I had passed my quarry."

Pulling out of the attack he found himself south of a group of Ju.87s flying apparently unmolested toward the coast.

"It looked like the Stukas were about to attack their target. Banking, I began my pursuit. It only took a few moments for me to reach the formation. My diving attack caused them to scatter and I latched onto one of them and fired the remainder of my ammunition at him.

"Smoke immediately began to trail from the dive bomber. The Stuka went into a steep dive, I followed. Suddenly, I realised this was foolish and began to take evasive action. The last I saw of the enemy aircraft was that it was still diving toward the channel."

Sgt Wolton returned to Warmwell, where he learnt that the third member of the section, Plt. Off. Deanesly, was missing. The Dornier crashed near Weymouth, but Deanesly's Spitfire was hit and he was forced to ditch in the sea wounded. He was rescued, but his injuries kept him from the Squadron for some weeks.

On the same day, Plt. Off. Dudley Williams was in action on three occasions. Moreover, in the month that followed he would log 34 sorties, including 16 scrambles and 13 patrols, attacking Me.109s on 11 August when his section escorted a Blenhiem of 604 Sqdn., based at Middle Wallop, to search for a missing aircraft over the Channel. On this day Fighter Command's entire front was stretched to the limit.

The action for 10 Group began in mid-morning as a raid massing over the French coast was plotted on radar before crossing the Channel. Initial diversionary feints were dealt with by 11 Group as the already alert 10 Group controller realised that the naval installations at Portland (which were to endure more assaults than any other target except London or Liverpool) were to be the objective.

Defending squadrons had already been moved forward to meet the onslaught, the Controller scrambling five squadrons to intercept, including 152 Sqdn., which was to lose Plt. Off. Jones. He was seen to extract himself from combat with a number of Me.109s and bale out, but he drowned before he could be rescued. This massive protracted action cost Middle Wallop's 238 Sqdn. the loss of four pilots. However, it was not until darkness that 152 Sqdn. would finally be stood down, affording the weary ground staff the opportunity to repair the machines, working with little respite late into the night, assisted by fitters, armourers and riggers from the training unit and Station workshop staff.

12 August 1940 would prove to be a day of further loss and some jubilation for Warmwell's fighters. 152 Sqdn., vectored with 609 Sqdn. to defend the Ventnor radar site, arrived to pounce on the raiders as they attempted to extricate themselves from the target

152 Squadron.
P/O Dudley Williams shot down four enemy aircraft and shared in the in-destruction of a fifth fighter whilst serving with 152 Squadron.
Cooke/Williams

area, claiming five enemy aircraft destroyed and two damaged. Plt. Off. Shepley and the experienced Australian, Flt. Lt Withall, failed to return, losses the unit could ill afford.

Warmwell's Spitfires were again tested the following day when Flg. Off. Inness of 152 Sqdn. was wounded in combat off Portland as sortie followed sortie. Desperate, its resources stretched, Fighter Command fought on tirelessly. By midday on 16 August all three fighter Groups were strained to the limit defending the Command's vital airfields. Tangmere, Biggin Hill, Kenley, Croydon and West Malling all received attacks. Vastly out-numbered, the Hurricanes and Spitfires harried and wreaked havoc amongst the huge formations of enemy bombers and their defending fighter screen, but as the aerial battles moved west Ford and Thorney Island came under threat.

10 Group's controller was quick to recognise the threatening situation and dispatched 152 and 234 Sqdns. Almost simultaneously from 11 Group 601, 43 and 602 Sqdns. were scrambled to block the enemy's escape. It could therefore only be a matter of time before Warmwell, which had resounded to numerous alerts, would receive direct attention. 25 August turned out to be the day of reckoning.

At teatime, catching a few moments of tense relaxation, 152 Sqdn.'s fatigued groundstaff and pilots were about to bite into their often rushed staple diet of a wads washed down with a mug of tea as the order to scramble was yelled across the dispersal. Roaring into the air, the squadron raced to meet, advancing on Portland, a massed formation which, as it approached the coast, began to break off into attack formations.

Scrambled from Exeter, 87 Sqdn. converged on the enemy, joined by 609 and 17 Sqdn., the Spitfires and Hurricanes throwing up a formidable defensive screen. Meanwhile on the ground the 14th LAA Regiment, dispersed around Warmwell's defensive perimeter, engaged the enemy. It was inevitable that some of the bombers would break through, and damage was sustained across the domestic site and on the airfield itself, where aircraft and hangars were damaged. The sick quarters, only recently protected by a blast bank, received a direct hit, and medical records drifted on the summer air as Warmwell's outside communications were severed for several hours.

Defending their base, 152 Sqdn. pilots were in the thick of the action, joining squadrons from Tangmere, Middle Wallop and Exeter. Luckily Warmwell did not suffer any casualties on the ground but its Spitfire squadron lost Plt. Offs. Hogg and Wildblood in the girating mass of vapour trails reeling above the heads of those taking cover in slit trenches, their cheering rising above the crescendo of exploding bombs as an enemy aircraft was seen to trail smoke.

Within minutes the defenders were returning, wind whistling through their gunports as they landed and taxied to a halt. Ground crews leapt from cover to refuel and re-arm the machines.

In the immediate aftermath, personnel not actively engaged in the turn-round of fighters were active with spades, filling in the craters and marking the unexploded bombs. That night, although not as a direct result of the Warmwell assault but retaliating to the bombing of London, Bomber Command attacked Berlin. By the second week of September Warmwell's fighters would be requested to help defend the nation's capital.

The task of clearing up continued overnight and into the next day, which proved not as frantic as the previous one, with few combat encounters, unlike the following day's clashes, during which Flg. Off. O'Brian and Plt. Off. Beaumont destroyed a He.111, resulting

152 Squadron.
The Squadron's dispersal hut. On the edge of the photograph can be seen the 'crash or blood
wagon' ready in case of emergency.
Cooke/Williams

in the latter ditching in the Channel. Meanwhile, at Middle Wallop, 1 September witnessed a change of fighter units when 234 and 249 Sqdns. arrived, ready to join the battle over London, the eastern counties and the hostile Channel. It was during one such operation that 152 Sqdn. lost Sgt. Barker, and on 23 September Plt. Off. Beaumont failed to return.

In constant action the strain was beginning to show. Many of the original pilots who had flown to Warmwell from Acklington were dead, missing or in hospital; likewise for the ground crews, there was no respite in the desperate see-saw aerial battles. However, the action moved westward toward 10 Group's front on 25 September. By mid-morning Group was undecided what the target was to be, as the massed formation approaching the coast began to separate. Portland once more reeled under attack, but although it was believed that the objective was the Westland factory at Yeovil the enemy side-stepped and moved north to attack Filton while the defenders searched an empty sky. Perhaps misled by their ease of approach, the return was to be a different story for the enemy pilots, who had to literally fight their way out over Somerset, Devon and Dorset. The action cost 152 Squadron the loss of Sgts. Silver and Holland and forced the CO, Sqdn. Ldr. Devitt, to make an emergency landing near Bath.

This raid revealed a weakness in 10 Group defences which was remedied by the immediate transfer from Hendon of 501 Sqdn. to Filton.

On 26 September 152 Sqdn. suffered a further casualty when Sgt. Christie failed to return from combat.

Next day, 27 September, was a day of tremendous activity for 10 Group. Brand was ready, deploying five squadrons to engage the Filton-bound raid, during which 152 Sqdn. sustained five damaged machines. The population of Dorchester watched in horror as a Spitfire and a Me.110 collided, killing Plt. Off. Miller of 609 Sqdn.

Caught out by the intensity of the recent activity, both 10 and 11 Groups were prepared for the mid-afternoon contest on 30 September as the Westland aircraft factory at Yeovil became the target in a heated engagement that began over Weymouth. The raid was initially met by 56 Sqdn. from Boscombe Down and 152 Sqdn., which was to lose Sgt. Reddington, fighting to check the enemy's advance as 504 Sqdn. joined the throng above drifting cloud. Bombing blind, the raiders released their bombs over Sherborne, causing numerous casualties in the ancient abbey town.

A change in the weather and an autumnal breeze left a chill in the air as 152 Sqdn.'s few remaining old hands chalked up their flying and combat hours. Like Sgt. Wolton, most decided to remain aloof and not to become too friendly with replacement pilots. The emotional strain was intense, none more so than when newly promoted Plt. Off. Akroyd died on 7 October in yet another hard fought action. His Spitfire crashed near Dorchester, where he was transferred to hospital but succumbed to his injuries. In the same fight 609 Sqdn. lost Sgt. Feary, who, nursing his shot-up Spitfire, tried desperately to make it to Warmwell but was forced to abandon his fighter while too low for his parachute to deploy.

The remainder of October would prove little different, a mixture of deteriorating weather and numerous scrambles that had to be endured, often in atrocious conditions. One scramble resulted in the loss of Sgt. Shepperd, who, while vainly searching for base on 18

152 Squadron.
Sgt. J. McBride Christie lost his life over the Channel in an engagement with Me.109 fighters.
His body was recovered from the sea and buried in his native Scotland.
Cooke/Williams

October, released his seat harness and leaned over the cockpit side in an attempt to see the ground. His Spitfire probably clipped some trees, causing the machine to career through wooded undergrowth to come to rest in marshy ground. Its wreckage was scattered over a large area, revealing a distressing sight for the recovery party which was dispatched to convey the pilot's remains to Warmwell.

British and German accounts differ regarding the end of the Battle of Britain, the Luftwaffe maintaining that the fighting did not cease until the Spring of 1941, but nevertheless some sharp actions were fought in the closing weeks of 1940. The most notable was on 28 November, when 609 Sqdn., taking its rotational turn at Warmwell, was scrambled late in the afternoon. This was followed almost immediately by 152 Sqdn. to intercept a high level incursion led by Maj. Helmut Wieck, Geshwaderkommodore of JG 2. Climbing flat out, the Spitfires saw some of the vapour trail cease, and moments later Wieck's section smashed through them, scattering both squadrons.

Each squadron lost two pilots in the encounter, in which Wieck was posted missing. The credit passed to Flt. Lt. J Dundas, whom it is presumed shot the German ace down due to an R/T transmission of victory, received before he too became a casualty. However, neither side could produce an actual witness to the Geshwaderdommodore's fate.

Next day 609 Sqdn. moved from Middle Wallop to become residents at Warmwell. On 152 Sqdn. most of the original pilots who had moved with the unit from Northumberland had now been posted to other duties, and the Station looked forward to the New Year.

152 Squadron.
P/O Watson would survive the Battle of Britain but became a casualty in the action of 28 November 1940, during one of the closing air battles of that year.
Cooke/Williams

1941

On the first day of the new year, snow fell but four days later Pilot Officer Marrs of 152 Squadron despatched an unidentified enemy aircraft into the sea off Weymouth. Bad weather conditions persisted throughout the month and more snow fell in February, once again making the airfield unserviceable. On 24th February 609 Sqdn. departed for operations in 11 Group as 234 Sqdn. Moved forward from St Eval.

In March, 152 Sqdn. was again in combat and 234 Sqdn. engaged and destroyed an enemy machine over the Channel on the 11th. 234 Sqdn. also made some limited daylight offensive sorties on coastal targets in Northern France. In addition, Sqdn. Ldr. Gleed led four Hurricanes of 87 Sqdn. from Exeter to Warmwell on 15th March to begin the first of a number of night intruder missions. Eleven days later, on 26th March, Warmwell received a visit from the Luftwaffe, but no damage or casualties were reported.

All Fools Day, 1st April, dawned with low cloud and squally rain showers which grounded all aircraft over most of the south west. Moments after 1225 hours, three low flying enemy aircraft, passing from east to west, wreaked havoc as they machine gunned and bombed the domestic site and working areas of the airfield. In their wake, they left numerous casualties. Some were killed instantly. A few fought their injuries, but finally succumbed and died during the three days following the raid. Many other personnel received serious wounds from which, in some cases, they took months to recover. The diary for the CGS recorded that 40 bombs were dropped, seven of them of a delayed action type which were defused over the next two days, including one in a controlled explosion.

All Fools Day 1941.
Warmwell, like all of 10 Group was stood down, all flying was cancelled until the weather improved, however 3 German bombers crossed the coast and followed the railway line to Wool then cut across land and devastated Warmwell causing considerable damage to the airfield and the domestic site, including numerous wounded and fatal casualties.
Cooke/Wilford

152 Squadron.
Spitfire UM-R, smaller codes have been applied in comparison to UM-N. The photograph was
probably taken in the spring of 1941, shortly before the squadron left Warmwell for Portreath.
Cooke/Williams

234 Squadron.
Presented by the people of Weston-Super-Mare, Spitfire P7925 was frequently flown by P/O
Wilford.
Cooke/Wilford

Hurricanes of 87 Squadron moved forward to Warmwell to fly limited night intruder missions in the late Spring of 1941. Flg. Off. R. P. Beamont participated in these missions.
Photo: Beamont

A Wings for Victory parade marching up Weymouth Avenue in Dorchester. The brick building in the background is the Police Station.
Cooke

One Spitfire was totally destroyed and a number of aircraft severely damaged, the main hangar and workshop offices were destroyed, and further damage was sustained to one of the Bellman hangars. Luckily, a bomb which crashed through the roof of the crowded NAAFI failed to detonate! The sudden sound of bombs exploding and the chatter of machine-gun fire alerted Sgt. Kearsey and two pilots of 152 Sqdn. who were at readiness at their dispersal. Pounding to their fighters, they took off in immediate pursuit, but the enemy aircraft disappeared into the cloud, and although the Spitfires received a number of vectors the enemy aircraft made good their escape.

As a direct result of the raid morale suffered in the days immediately following, as funeral processions marched to Holy Trinity Church in the nearby village of Warmwell. 152 Sqdn received advance warning that a move to Portreath on 9 April was planned. Warmwell had become very popular where the Luftwaffe was concerned, as on 24 April eight more bombs fell within the confines of the Station and caused damage to nearby civilian property.

On 7 May the Station was on its best behaviour to receive the C-in-C Fighter Command, Air Marshall W S Douglas, who came to inspect 234 Sqdn. Two days later the Luftwaffe returned under the cover of darkness, as it would for the next three consecutive nights. Meanwhile, on 13 May, 234 Sqdn. lost two pilots in a collision off the French coast and on the 19th two more Spitfires were lost defending a convoy, to which the enemy returned later in the day. This time the squadron was waiting, claiming five enemy aircraft and one 'probable' for the loss of two additional Spitfires; luckily both pilots were saved. Losses were further avenged in June when the squadron destroyed two enemy aircraft over the sea.

Meanwhile, advance parties of the Central Gunnery School had left Warmwell on 26 June for Castle Kennedy in Scotland.

Wing Operations

So far the war for Fighter Command had been a defensive action, numerous airfields being enlarged and new ones such as Ibsley, just north of Ringwood, becoming operational. Plans were now laid for offensive operations, for which those airfields large enough would support a fighter Wing. Meanwhile 13 Sqdn., which had flown anti-invasion patrols from Warmwell throughout the summer of 1940 as well as many searches over the sea for missing pilots, supplied a cadre of personnel to form the Warmwell detachment of 276 (ASR) Sqdn. At Ibsley the Middle Wallop Wing was being galvanised together under the leadership of Wg. Cdr. Ian 'Widge' Gleed to comprise 234, 118 and 501 Sqdns., while at Warmwell on 6 November 402 Squadron RCAF arrived equipped with Hurricane Mk *IIbs* to begin limited offensive operations against enemy shipping.

Since the departure of the CGS the ranges had been fairly quiet, but the facilities were soon put to good use as 10 Group opened its own armament practice camp by reforming the Target Towing Flight to service a succession of squadrons.

The ground defence provided by the Dorset regiment changed in September as elements of 70th YS (Young Service) Battalion of the regiment replaced the former sections.

402 R.C.A.F. Squadron.
Pilots from the squadron line up for the camera. To avoid confusion with similarly numbered R.A.F. squadrons all Canadian squadrons were issued with a unit number in the 400 series; thus 2 Squadron R.C.A.F. became 402 R.C.A.F. Squadron and as such became one of the first fighter-bomber squadrons equipped with Hurricane IIb machines capable of carrying two underwing mounted bombs.
Cooke/Murchie

175 Squadron.
Hurricane IIb BP737 returning to Warmwell after unloading its practice bombs over the Chesil Beach range.
Author's collection

A month later two young soldiers were killed when a Hurricane of 32 Sqdn. crashed into one of the huts used by the regiment. Meanwhile a further change of command took place when Gp. Capt. Boyd became the new Station Commander and at the same time 276 Sqdn. became fully operational. November, all in all, was a very busy month, rounded off when 402 Sqdn. and escorts attacked Morlaix airfield.

December for 402 Sqdn. was spent over the ranges or on dreary convoy patrols. January 1942 proved no different except for one or two brushes with enemy fighters and a collision by two of the squadron's Hurricanes, from which both pilots survived.

On 10 February the Ibsley Wing escorted four of the squadron's Hurribombers to fruitlessly search for an enemy destroyer, possibly moving west to join the armada which escorted the Scharnhorst, Prinze Eugen and Gneisenau as they made an audacious dash up the channel on the night of 11/12 February.

When the British finally woke up to what was happening it was too late, Operation Fuller was put into immediate effect, and 402 Sqdn. was ordered forward to Manston to join the massive but futile attempt to stop the capital ships by naval and air attack. The air umbrella put up by the Luftwaffe and the defending naval flotilla was impenetrable and a heroic but suicidal attack led by Lt. Cmdr. Eugene Esmonde, who was to be posthumously awarded the V.C. was annihilated. 42 British aircraft were lost in this abysmal operation. 402 Sqdn. was not deployed and returned to base late that evening. On the morning of the 12th, the Luftwaffe visited a number of south coast airfields, including Warmwell and

Exeter.

Four days after the debacle of Operation Fuller, on 16 February, a reconnaissance aircraft spotted a German flotilla moving west at the extreme end of the Channel. 402 Sqdn. was ordered to Perranporth to rendezvous with their escorts and soon were racing over the sea at 300 feet. Closing on the flotilla, the Hurricanes immediately gained height and turned into the attack, meeting a wall of flak. The escorting Spitfires immediately broke away and raked the ships with machine-gun fire as the Hurribombers dived to within a few hundred feet of their targets before releasing their bombs. When they left the flotilla one destroyer had been sunk and three others damaged. Jubilant, they returned to Warmwell next day.

The remainder of February saw little activity except for a further sea sweep in which the Hurricanes failed to make contact. That day advance orders were received to prepare to move.

A New Squadron

Leaving their Hurribombers behind, 402 Sqdn. left for Colerne on 4 March, but next day a number of the Canadians received orders to return to Warmwell to join 175 Sqdn., then being formed by Sqdn. Ldr. Smith. A few days later Smith was posted and Flt. Lt. Pennington-Legh assumed command – the squadron becoming operational on 2 April.

Ground staff and new pilots continued to arrive throughout the month as the former Squadron's Hurricanes were repainted to replace the 'AE' fuselage codes of 402 Sqdn. with 175 Squadron's 'HH'.

On 16 April 175 Sqdn. carried out its first offensive operation by bombing Maupertus airfield, from which one Hurricane failed to return. Unfortunately, three ASR patrols failed to find the missing pilot. The remainder of the month was spent on local flying and convoy protection patrols but on the 25th Maupertus once more received attention.

Five days later, having moved to Portreath the previous day, eight Hurribombers and escorting Spitfires attacked an enemy convoy, damaging the destroyer escorts in a hotly contested operation. Much of the month of May was spent on exercises, tedious convoy patrols and local flying but on the 15th the squadron, with the Ibsley Wing, carried out a very successful shipping attack off Cap de la Hague, sinking one destroyer and damaging two others, which were believed sunk after the Hurricanes had departed.

175 Squadron.
S/L Pennington-Legh (second left) with A Flight under the trees of Knighton Woods. The squadron comprised of many pilots from the Commonwealth.
Cooke/Murchie

June was no different – much boredom interspersed with hectic action against shipping targets. Maupertus was once more attacked early in the month and the squadron claimed two Ju.88s shot down off Portland on the 9th, but the highlight of the month was when four aircraft attacked eight minesweepers off the French coast, encountering what Flt. Lt. Murchie RCAF described in his flying log as "Red hot intense flak". A few days later a two aircraft section destroyed a possible flak ship.

July provided further shipping attacks and a major strike on the 30th; the squadron immediately returned to the target area but failed to relocate the ships.

Operation Jubilee

On 6 August the squadron moved to Bolt Head for a shipping strike, returning to base three days later. Meanwhile the on/off plans for an attack on Dieppe were finally given the green light for what was to turn into a disaster. Led by Sqdn. Ldr. Pennington-Legh, the squadron moved forward to RAF Ford on 16 August to join its sister unit, 174, Sqdn. Those remaining at Warmwell were totally 'in the dark' as to where the squadron was and what they were doing.

Awoken early on the morning of 19 August, the pilots were briefed on the operation and their respective targets while the armada of ships was slowly approaching Dieppe under the cover of darkness. At Ford, overcrowding was most evident as machines from various squadrons were involved in taxiing collisions as they prepared to take off.

175 Sqdn. pilots, ordered to attack the Goering Artillery Battery and the German Divisional Headquarters at Arques, were led on their first sortie by Sqdn. Ldr. Pennington-Legh. Eight Hurribombers climbed into the pre-dawn gloom, passing over the naval flotilla unseen below.

As dawn broke the pilots gained altitude and located their targets, encountering intense flak and anti-aircraft fire as they dived upon the gun positions, partially obscured by drifting smoke which effectively concealed the target from view, with the result that the effectiveness of the strike was unconfirmed. Flt. Lt. Murchie, instructed to destroy the German HQ, failed to pinpoint his objective and eventually bombed an unidentified gun position. His No. 2 was more successful and located the HQ, but was unable to confirm the results as drifting smoke from the raging ground battle effectively obscured the area.

All eight machines returned safely to Ford which was a hive of activity. Minutes after being de-briefed they were preparing for a second strike to take place mid-morning.

On the beach at Dieppe the situation was growing more desperate by the minute, but 175 Sqdn., briefed to attack gun position Rommel, took off to rendezvous with its escorts and 87 Sqdn. which would follow up their attack.

Climbing, the Hurricanes levelled off, crossed the coast and dived, hurtling their bombs into the target area. Flames were seen to rise as they pulled out amid very intense defensive fire, which hit Sgt. Conroy's aircraft as he came out of his attack.

During the battle the squadron engaged a number of enemy aircraft, ending the day claiming a He 111 and one Fw. 190 as 'probables' and a further 190 as damaged. Meanwhile Sgt. Conroy was forced to abandon his Hurricane 10 miles off the coast, but rescue was at hand and he was taken on board the Polish destroyer Slazak.

The ground operation was now in dire circumstances; few of the Commandos were able to achieve their objectives and were slaughtered on the beach. Casualties rose alarmingly and the decision to withdraw was finally taken. For 175 Sqdn. the day's activities were over, but the RAF would continue to cover the withdrawal.

For the remainder of August the squadron attended 10 Group APC, the attachment lasting into September, which proved to be a relatively quiet month after the action over Dieppe. October began with the inevitable convoy patrols as advance orders were received to prepare to move on 10 October to Harrowbeer.

First Americans

1942 would witness numerous squadron movements attending the APC. Notable in July was the 307th Fighter Squadron, 31st Fighter Group, 8th Air Force.

The 31st was the first USAAF fighter unit to be posted to the U.K. comprising of three fighter squadrons - the 307th, 308th and the 309th. It was soon followed by the 52nd Fighter Group and, or course, thousands of other fighter pilots and bomber crews that formed the nucleus of the American fighter and heavy bomber offensive that would be operating from Britain.

Whilst on home soil the 31st was designated as a Pursuit Group but when the unit arrived in Britain it was re-appointed as a Fighter Group along the lines of RAF units, as it would operate under RAF control until such times as the embryo 8th Air Force became fully operational. At home in the States, the Group flew the Bell P 39 Airacobra. This was a radically designed fighter aircraft in which the engine was fitted centrally in the fuselage behind the pilot's seat, transmitting the power from the engine to the propeller via a shaft which ran through the cockpit.

The British ordered the aircraft but the P.39s supplied to the RAF were found to be lacking in performance power and would, therefore, be at a distinct disadvantage when pitted against the Luftwaffe's current fighter aircraft. The type would equip only one RAF squadron - 601 squadron - which operated the P.39 for seven months from September 1941 until March 1942 when it was re-equipped with Spitfires.

The 31st F.G. was initially based at RAF Atcham in Shropshire and equipped with Spitfires, in a form of reverse lease-lend as the 8th Air Force had yet to equip the embryo units arriving in the U.K. The first machines received by the Group were 'time expired'

Lt. J. Cooper 307th Fighter Squadron, 31st Fighter Group. 8th U.S.A.A.F.
Cooke/Turk

Spitfire Mk IIs but these were soon replaced with Mk Vb aircraft shortly before the 307th Fighter Squadron flew to Warmwell to attend the 10 Group APC on July 21st 1942; their ground echelon travelling by road. At this date none of the pilots had yet been subjected to the rigours of combat and so Warmwell's instructors had to ensure that the ground crews were trained in the turn around of their aircraft under operational conditions and that pilots experienced the expenditure of live ammunition. The attachment involved numerous theoretical lectures interspersed between air-ground live firing exercises along the Chesil ranges and camera gun attacks. Nine days later, on July 30th, the 307th returned briefly to Atchams, packed their kit and flew to Biggin Hill to operate under the auspices of 11 Group Fighter Command, where the Group participated in a number of offensive operations, including the Dieppe fiasco.

The sister squadrons of the 307th also attended other armament practice camps before they, too, returned to Atchams and service within 11 Group. In August the 31st Fighter Group bade their Spitfire Vs farewell and boarded ship to an unknown destination. On board then learnt that it was sailing to the Miditerranean, where it received further Spitfires and participated in the North African and Italian campaigns.

Of Whirlwinds and Typhoons

263 Squadron.
Sgt. S. Beaumont was responsible for the 'Gremlin' painted on his machine and other work found on the wall of Tree Stores Crossways, which during the war was the YMCA hostel.
Cooke/Oliver

Arriving from Colerne on 7 September, 263 Sqdn. Whirlwinds taxied to their dispersal. The aircraft, recently converted to carry bombs, would, with 175 Sqdn. become the only fighter-bomber squadrons operating within 10 Group.

Next day, escorted by the Exeter Wing, 263 Sqdn. carried out its first Roadstead operation, searching in vain for its target. 24 hours later, in company with the Ibsley Wing, success was at hand when four armed trawlers were attacked and two sunk off Cap de la Hague. The remainder of the month passed in relative boredom, the monotony only broken by anti-Rhubarb patrols, shipping reconnaissance sorties and one or two scrambles.

October followed a similar pattern except for the 3rd. Four machines led by the CO were dispatched to attack shipping in Alderney Harbour, but two miles from the harbour Sqdn. Ldr. Woodward's Whirlwind was hit by intense and accurate anti-aircraft fire, forcing him to break off his attack and limp back to base on one engine. Meanwhile the three remaining aircraft went into the attack, a further Whirlwind sustaining damage, but all four reached Warmwell without further incident. For the remainder of the month a number of armed reconnaissance patrols were made and the inevitable shipping and coastal convoy patrols continued into November, the monotony eventually being broken by a Rhubarb operation against a rail target in the Valognes-Carentan area from which Plt. Off. Gill failed to return.

The squadron returned to the same area on the 16th and also attacked an E-boat off the coast. Three days later a Roadstead from Predannack produced no results as the weather deteriorated rapidly, but on 7 December a shipping attack resulted in the loss of a further experienced pilot.

On the preceding day, 6 December, however, a Vickers Wellington Mk II bomber flew over the Chesil ranges. Approaching low over the Fleet Lagoon the bomber released a half scale version of a device designed by Dr. Barnes Wallis which it was anticipated would richochet off the surface and bounce over the water of the lagoon. Frustratingly, the trials proved a failure, not only did the bombs fail to bounce, they often disintegrated. Further sorties continued over the coming weeks but a veil of secrecy surrounded the project and the modifications undertaken to the Wellington in the station workshops as the project progressed. Finally, the team were rewarded with success and full sized versions of the bombs constructed, but for this purpose the Chesil Range and the Wellington were deemed inadequate and the project left Warmwell. On the night of 16/17 May 1943, 617 Squadron led by W/C Guy Gibson VC successfully attacked the Rhur dams and passed into history.

Meanwhile, on 14 December two Whirlwinds of 263 Sqdn. were dispatched on a sweep but failed to locate their target. As the fighter-bombers re-crossed the Channel they were instructed to change course and were vectored to intercept two Fw 190s returning to their French base. In the ensuing combat one enemy aircraft was claimed as damaged but

Bouncing bomb. For approximately forty years this spherical object lay on the shore of the Fleet opposite the Chesil ranges. Few people knew or realised its historic importance as being one of 'stores' dropped by Dr. Barnes Wallis during the Bouncing Bomb trials in December 1942. Cooke

A 263 Squadron Whirlwind, its armament was formidable. The CO suspected that ground staff knew little of the unit's operational function, he arranged a film show of camera-gun film showing the destructive power of the aircraft's armament.
Cooke/Oliver

A Typhoon of 266 Squadron protected by a revetment on the western boundary of Warmwell airfield.
Cooke

lack of fuel forced the Whirlwinds to break off the engagement and return to Warmwell.

January 1943 saw little activity but in February there was a change, as night attacks were commenced. On one of these Sgt. Williams was forced to ditch in the channel and a few days later a further Whirlwind was lost in an exercise with the army.

Towards the end of the month Maupertus received 263 Sqdn.'s attention on three consecutive days, but orders had been received to move: 'A' Flight to Harrowbeer and 'B' Flight to Fairwood Common; but on 14 March 1943 the complete Squadron returned to Warmwell. A month later the new control tower, constructed to Air Ministry design 12779/41, was brought into use. Before this all air traffic movements had been controlled by a duty pilot and crew.

266 Sqdn. had begun to receive Typhoons during January 1942 at Duxford, but for the next few months the squadron would be non-operational as the unit fought to overcome the engine and structural failures from which the Typhoon was suffering. Unfortunately these problems persisted and were still being experienced when the squadron arrived at Warmwell on 18 September to carry out limited operational sorties.

On that day the squadron diarist recorded that he was looking forward to the move to Warmwell in the hope of seeing more action, but bad weather prevented the departure from Duxford until late afternoon. Upon arrival a section was placed on immediate readiness. From then until the end of the month the unit flew numerous patrols and scrambles and received many vectors to combat an increasing menace from enemy fighter-bombers attacking south coast towns.

October opened with the boredom of riding cover to a convoy, but as the month progressed shipping reconnaissance sorties were flown, often proving fruitless. Various vectors were received, but engagements were few, and engine reliability remained a severe problem, causing one machine to make a wheels-up landing on the airfield on 8 November. A further Typhoon was lost twenty days later when it crashed near Ibsley, but a deterioration of the weather greatly limited the Squadron's activities during December. Sqdn. Ldr. Green and his No.2 flew a Rhubarb sortie on the 23rd intending to attack rail locomotives, but low cloud over France forced their early return. Returning to the same area on 31 December, the CO led six Typhoons on a successful mission, claiming a number of locomotives damaged.

After a huge 'bash' thrown in the mess on New Year's Eve, the first day of 1943 brought disappointment rather than joy, as the squadron was informed that it would be succeeded at Warmwell by 257 Sqdn., similarly equipped with Typhoons. 266 Sqdn. flew its last scramble on 4 January and two days later roared into the air over the trees of Knighton Woods to replace 257 Sqdn. at Exeter.

Inclement weather made Warmwell unserviceable for much of January 1943, so 257 Sqdn. detached aircraft to Ibsley for possible operations. From its home base there was little flying until 5 February, when 'B' Flight carried out a Rhubarb in the Bayeux region, attacking one locomotive. The unserviceability of Warmwell restricted the squadron's activities to the boredom of standing patrols to intercept fighter-bomber incursions and sorties escorting the ASR Flight.

Unfortunately the tedium of repeated standing patrols throughout the hours of daylight chafed at the patience of 257 Sqdn. pilots in the early days of March. Much of the airfield was still unserviceable when Flt. Lt. Miller was killed while attempting to avoid another aircraft when srambled in the early evening of 8 March.

The tedium was further compounded on 14 March when 263 Sqdn. returned to Warmwell, immediately taking part in a Circus operation whilst all the Typhoon pilots could do was to watch in frustration the aggressive activities of the Whirlwinds, which on three consecutive days from 20 March attacked the Marlaix Viaduct and other targets.

Roadsteads and Circus operations followed throughout April. Ten Whirlwinds were dispatched to attack Guipavas airfield on 13 April, escorted by the Portreath Wing; later the same day Sgt. Macauley failed to return from a four aircraft shipping strike. Three days later a further Whirlwind was lost, and during the night of 17/18 April three machines failed to return to base. Further hazardous shipping strikes took place on 28 April, when four Whirlwinds led by Flt. Lt. Geoff Warnes located a convoy, causing havoc amongst the ships.

257 Sqdn. finally had cause for jubilation on 7 April when Flg. Off. Stieb destroyed an Me.109 south of the Isle of Wight. Meanwhile there was little change in the Squadron's activities or fortunes. Engine reliability, still causing concern, forced Plt. Off. Lao to make an emergency landing on 10 April and three days later another Typhoon glided back to the Station to make a deadstick landing. On 14 April a two-aircraft patrol intercepted a couple of Me.109s, despatching one and claiming the other as a 'probable'.

263 Squadron's popular commander S/L Geoff Warnes (left) with one of the unit's flight commanders F/L Holmes. S/L Warnes was a charismatic leader and much respected by both pilots and ground staff. Sadly he lost his life after baling out over the Channel later in the war. Cooke/Oliver

Neither squadron had anything to show for its activities for two weeks, but 257 Sqdn. threw a fair 'binge' during the middle of the month to celebrate three years of operational life. Meanwhile the Whirlwinds attacked Cherbourg harbour on 14 April. A few days later two Whirlwinds had a snap engagement with a couple of Fw.190s and on the night of 21/22 April the Squadron sank a motor vessel off Cherbourg. Next day, escorted by their friends from Ibsley, four Whirlibombers attacked a convoy off Guernsey, but intense defensive fire obscured the results and one Whirlwind had to limp back to Warmwell.

Whirlwind losses and damage on operations were now causing concern. In late May the squadron was down to five serviceable machines, but the problem was soon to be resolved when 263 Sqdn.'s sister unit, 137 Sqdn., which was to re-equip with Hurricanes, transferred its Whirlwinds to 263 Sqdn., to the delight of the pilots. However, it was not until 15 June that the next offensive shipping strike took place, resulting in the loss of Plt. Off. Cotton. That day, Sqd. Ldr. Baker bade farewell, the popular Geoff Warnes assumed command, and the squadron was stood down for a short period by moving to Zeals.

257 Sqdn. had some further success by intercepting and destroying a Fw.190 which had attacked Torquay on 30 May, but the squadron had to wait until 23 June for its next taste of action. Joining with 183 and 266 Sqdns., the Typhoons bombed Maupertus, but engine serviceability was now severe and only seven of the squadron's Typhoons were operational! Meanwhile the arrival on 19 June of rocket-firing Hurricane IVs of 164 Sqdn. did little to boost the latter squadron's aggressive spirit, the prohibited use of their secret rocket projectiles over enemy-held territory severely curtailing its operational aspirations.

A return visit by 257 Sqdn. to Maupertus was made on 10 July. Two days later 263 Sqdn. returned to Warmwell, but July produced little or no activity, although 257 Sqdn. escorted the Hurricanes of 164 Sqdn. on an abortive shipping reconnaissance on the 27th.

Eight Whirlwinds joined a Circus operation to Guipavas airfield escorted by both the Ibsley and Portreath Wings, although 257 Sqdn.'s efforts to get to grips with the enemy were still lacking in fulfillment. The only redeeming operation before the squadron left for Beaulieu on 16 August was with other squadrons escorting Bostons to attack the U-Boat works west of Renneson on the 8th.

Sqdn. Ldr. Baker, who had resumed command of 263 Sqdn, when the unit returned in July, led a successful strike against E-boats on 11 August and participated in a Circus operation four days later. 164 Sqdn. had departed on 5 August but for 263 Sqdn. the remainder of the month saw little action. Meanwhile 10 Group APC at Warmwell was under review, the target towing flight being disbanded in September as the Whirlwinds were transferred to 11 Group for a short period of operations.

The first week of October saw little activity, but as the month progressed 263 Sqdn., now back at Warmwell, carried out some night attacks against rail targets and on 24 October twelve Whirlwinds were dispatched to raid the Munsterland docked in Cherbourg harbour, losing two machines. The Munsterland then became a prime target, to which the squadron returned on 28 and 30 October.

Ramrods were flown during the early part of November, followed by shipping strikes, claiming damaged surface craft on the 10th and more visits to the Munsterland on the 25th and 26th. However, the day of the Whirlwind was reaching its climax, and the squadron left on 5 December to convert to Typhoons.

The move back to Warmwell by 257 Sqdn. on 16 September was not popular.

Operations from southern airfields had been gradually slowing down and the squadron spent much of the remaining months of the year carrying out numerous standing patrols, a few escort sorties and Ramrod operations. The first casualty for two years was suffered on 31 October when two Typhoons aborted a Rhubarb operation and became separated on the homeward stretch, one of them failing to return to base.

Shipping reconnaissance's and limited Rhubarb operations continued through November, a moderately successful shipping strike mid-month helping to reduce the boredom as bad weather limited the unit's activities. Nevertheless the squadron celebrated Christmas in good style, but lost one of the squadron's Burmese pilots on 31 December when providing the escort on a Ramrod sweep.

The loss of Plt. Off. Yi greatly overshadowed the New Year celebrations. A number of search and rescue sorties flown on 1 January to locate him were unsuccessful and were called off when the chance of his survival was nil. On 4 January the squadron carried out its first Noball strike against V1 launching sites, followed by a further attack three days later, but the waterlogged airfield restricted operations until 14 January, when a third Noball sortie took place just as the squadron received advance notice to prepare to move to Beaulieu.

A period of limited flying activity preceded the arrival of advance parties of USAAF personnel to prepare the way for the eventual arrival of the 474th Fighter Group. Activity was mostly confined to squadrons using the ranges for armament practice, including 263 Sqdn., which had now re-equipped with Typhoons. The detachment of 276 (ASR) Sqdn. departed in April as the USAAF Fighter Group assumed command of the airfield, during which there was a fatal crash of one of 263 Sqdn's Typhoons when the pilot 'beat up' the airfield to impress the new arrivals.

Station 454, USAAF Moreton

In the months that followed, Dorset began to resemble an armed fortress. The county's population of under a quarter of a million people would, in the months preceding the Normandy Invasion, be swelled by the influx of 500,000 military personnel, mostly consisting of soldiers, sailors and airmen from the United States.

The Supermarine Walrus amphibious aircraft saved many lives whilst serving with 276 and 275 Air-Sea-Rescue Squadrons which operated from south coast airfields, including Warmwell. This crew flew with 275 Squadron during the D. Day period.
Cooke

At Weymouth, 40 Air Sea Rescue Marine Craft Unit was established and numerous large American camps were sited around the county. Streets in principle towns became a vast vehicle park, necessitating the implementation of a one-way traffic system for military vehicles, as the build up to D-Day gained momentum. At Warmwell, 275 (ASR) Sqdn. Replaced 276 Squadron, as the 474th FG worked tirelessly to become operational.

The 474th Fighter Group had been activated at Elgin Field, Florida, in January 1943, initially as a medium altitude bomber unit, but on disbandment the personnel were moved to Van Nuys air base, California, to form the cadre of a three-squadron Fighter Group under the command of Lt. Col. Clinton Wasem.

A little over a year later, in February 1944, the Group crossed the Atlantic, making landfall and disembarking the HQ unit and the 428th Sqdn. at Liverpool while the 429th and 430th Sqdns. docked at Glasgow. The Group finally arrived at Moreton railway station on 12 March.

Having de-trained, the men marched in bright sunlight to the airfield, where Col.

474th Fighter Group. The exact circumstances of this incident is not known, however the probable cause was failure of the Lightning's undercarriage.
Cooke/Hanson-Hickok

An officer and photographer from the Press Corp is interviewing a pilot from the 474th Fighter Group.
Cooke/Hanson-Hickok

Wasem, as senior officer in a much depleted RAF presence, assumed command of Station 454 USAAF Moreton, Warmwell's official American designation.

Assigned to the IX U.S. Air Force as a fighter-bomber unit, the Group had to wait two weeks before it received its first P-38J Lightning fighters. The new aircraft required modification to a fighter-bomber configuration, and some of the work took place at Warmwell while the remainder was undertaken by a service echelon.

Throughout March and April 1944 new personnel continued to be drafted to the Group, which was now engaged on an intensive 'work-up' programme. Its first offensive mission was to Mayenne on 25 April, but much to the chagrin of the Group the Luftwaffe failed to appear.

May began with fighter sweeps and a B-17 escort mission, but to date the Group's activities had not resulted in any combat encounters. This situation changed dramatically on the first mission of 7 May. Escorting B-26s over Mezileres, the Lightnings were bounced by Fw.190s, and in the frenzied dogfight that followed three P-38s were lost. Further similar operations continued throughout the month, and on the 13th the Group flew its longest escort mission to date, covering B-17s to their target in Denmark. As May continued various fighter-bomber missions were flown to attack targets in occupied France – operations which, unknown to the Group, were in direct support of the forthcoming invasion.

A poor quality but descriptive shot of one of the 474th F. G.'s later natural metal finished P.38s at Warmwell.
Cooke/Hanson-Hickok

474th Fighter Group Lt. Anthony Usas had completed six missions when he posed for this photograph with his ground crew shortly before his death on 22 May 1944. He is buried in the American Cemetery at Colleville/St. Laurent, France.
Cooke/Hanson-Hickok

The 474th Fighter Group Association retail postcards of three paintings depicting an aircraft from each of the three squadrons of the Group. 'MisChief' was flown by Lt. Gene Hickok. The picture was painted by the author.
Cooke/Hanson-Hickok

D-day, 6 June 1944

Early in June the Group's diarist recorded: "We daubed on our warpaint – big black and white stripes on our ships so our ground troops wouldn't shoot us down". Special briefings were given to officers who were at once confined to camp and forbidden to discuss the matter. Meanwhile, those officers who had not been briefed participated in a number of dive-bombing missions to destroy rail communications in the beach-head area.

The briefings of 5 June were in earnest, and everyone knew that the invasion was on when the Group took off to shepherd part of the huge invasion armada from Southampton water to the Cherbourg peninsula.

No one at Warmwell slept that night as they watched in awe as plane after plane, glider and tug, passed over, navigation lights glowing in the night sky. Wave after wave, many at less that 500 feet altitude roared overhead, the sound reverberating around the airfield.

Thus it continued for three solid hours, after which there was a short period of silence before the peace was broken as the first returning aircraft passed over, their formation ragged and broken, many trailing smoke and showing signs of damage. Flares punctured the early morning light as desperate transports came into the circuit and were guided down, waiting ambulances following each machine. Doc. Collins, the Group's senior Medical Officer, worked tirelessly, and medical facilities were stretched to the limit of endurance.

Shortly after daybreak on D-day the Group was airborne to attack a railway bridge

474th Fighter Group. Destination Berlin. These cooks of the 428th F.S. have chalked 'Berlin bound' on the windshield of the Jeep. Hours later the Group departed from Warmwell.
Cooke/Hanson-Hickok

across the Seine in direct support of the invasion forces, losing two Lightnings, including one flown by the CO of the 430th FS. Maj. Temple. Next day, D+1, the P-38s were once again flying missions supporting the ground troops in the immediate beach-head area, strafing German road and rail transport and communication installations.In the days that followed many similar missions were flown, including escorting C-47 transport aircraft towing Waco gliders to St Mere Englise. Meanwhile the Group suffered increased casualties, including Capt. Gee, who was taking part in his first mission on 22 June when he dived straight into the ground, his P-38 exploding on impact.

By 4 July, when at home their folks were celebrating Independence Day, the Group chalked up its 69th combat mission, a bombing and strafing attack on rolling stock in the Le Mans area. Similar operations continued throughout the remaining days of the month, culminating in a night intruder mission.

While across the Channel the Allies were fighting desperately to increase their foothold in Normandy, establishing airstrips in the beach-head area, the 474th FG. prepared to stand down from operations, flying a final mission from Warmwell on 5 August.

That day Col. Wasem returned command of the Station to the RAF, but this was not a happy occasion as friction ensued between the two air forces as RAF inspectors noted the condition of the Station and its facilities. While advance parties of the 474th FG. already in the beach-head area were preparing landing strip A11, Neuilly-la-Floret, for the Group's arrival, the bulk of the ground staff moved to a massive camp at Came, near Dorchester, before embarking at Weymouth as the aircraft were flown to the Continent.

17 and 14 APCs

The 2nd tactical Air Force, formed in November 1943 to provide air support for ground forces, comprised 83 and 84 Groups. Initially squadrons were co-ordinated on Wing Stations, which were later allocated numbers; thus the Kenley Wing became 127 Wing, home to a RCAF Spitfire Wing consisting of 403, 421 and later 416 Sqdns. of 83 Group.

Throughout the remaining months of 1943 and early 1944 the Wings spent much of their time providing escort cover on daylight bombing operations, including attacking coastal defences and V1 launching sites, the latter code named Noball. These were strikes in which 257 Sqdn. had participated, but the departure of the 474th FG. to A11 (Neuilly) left a void of inactivity at Warmwell. However, 9th Air Force transport aircraft ran a constant cross-Channel service transferring stores and equipment to the Continent, such flights continuing throughout September as the RAF presence gradually increased. Air-sea rescue cover was now provided by a detachment of 277 (ASR) Sqdn., 275 Sqdn. having left for Bolt Head as 17 Armament Practice Camp opened, commencing flying operations in the last week of September.

A second armament practice camp, 14 APC, was formed in November, and between them the two units serviced a progression of squadrons from 83 and 84 Groups of 2nd TAF. On average four squadrons a month arrived from their Continental bases, ostensibly to sharpen their gunnery skills. However, the attachments were seen to provide a well-earned break from the rigour of operations, although they were not without casualties, sometimes fatal.

By the end of the year ten squadrons had visited the APCs and enjoyed the various off duty engagements arranged for their relaxation, especially tours of local breweries in Dorchester and Blandford with free beer tasting proving exceptionally popular!

Across the Channel, where the beach-head was firmly established, the Allied advance and massive air superiority resulted in few fighter-to-fighter encounters, but the Luftwaffe still had some teeth left, as the Allied air forces were to experience in the early hours of 1 January 1945, when operation Bodenplatte took the RAF and USAAF totally by surprise.

443 Sqdn., until recently part of 144 Wing, had been transferred to 127 Wing, now operating from Evere, but escaped the debacle owing to its timely attachment to the Warmwell APC. Returning to Evere on 2 January, it was found that the airfield had sustained little damage to its facilities during the attack that could not easily be made good in the short term, including the loss of eleven Spitfires. Twelve more aircraft were damaged on the ground, but the balance was somewhat redressed when 443 Sqdn.'s sister unit, 403 Sqdn. claimed six of the attacking force.

Throughout January only three Squadrons attended the APC, and its activities were severely curtailed by heavy snow late in the month.

Typhoon, Tempest and Spitfire units of 83 and 84 Groups continued to fly to Warmwell until September 1945, but the Station had been living on borrowed time since victory was won in Europe. In the twelve months from September 1944 until closure more than forty Squadrons visited the APCs. On 3 October 17 APC's aircraft were flown to the Continent and its personnel were transferred or demobilised. Warmwell then became a forward airfield in the Colerne sector, but the closing of the Armament Practice Camps immediately resulted in the Station being reduced to a Care & Maintenance state. For a brief period it

V. J. Day. The station was already being run down when news of the Japanese surrender was received. A wild party followed in the gymnasium. The building has survived and is now the village hall of Crossways.

Cooke

became a satellite of Exeter, but Warmwell's operational life was over.

When the Japanese capitulated in August 1945 the final cessation of operations from Warmwell was gaining momentum but when the end came it was almost instantaneous – 17 APC closed within four days! A few RAF military police and personnel remained on the station to ensure that the airfield was secure whilst part of the camp became a demobilisation centre. Meanwhile, work began to prepare some of the living quarters to receive RAF service personnel and their families trapped abroad throughout the years of hostilities. All too soon, controversy returned within the corridors of power as decisions were made regarding the former airfield's future.

During the early 1950's and 1960s much of the Station remained, although the airfield itself was returned to agricultural use. Housing development gradually began to replace the decaying huts and the airfield became a source of gravel extraction and now resembles a lunar landscape. Little remains of the Station's former life except a few hardstandings, the two Bellman hangars constructed in 1940 and the control tower, which has been converted into a dwelling, standing sentinel over the quarry. For some years until the expansion of gravel extraction this formed part of Woodsford Farms. The scene made a sad sight for veterans of the 474th Fighter Group to behold in 1984, when they paid their first visit to their former base since their departure in 1944. Ten years on, when the veterans made a second pilgrimage, the passage of years had witnessed the destruction of a great deal more of the former airfield. In the intervening years, however, RAF Warmwell had been commemorated by the dedication of a Memorial Stone.

Now Crossways' Village Hall, this building had a multitude of uses during the life of the airfield. Hann

A Search for Answers

An archaeological excavation is, by definition, the destruction of all or part of an historical site. An archaeological investigation team will, however, through its meticulous recording of the material evidence, ensure that the information is preserved and documented for the future. The mention of a metal detector to a conventional archaeologist will probably bring forth a negative response. This is understandable when irresponsible individuals, armed with a detector, have destroyed vital archaeological evidence. Even the removal of seemingly insignificant artefacts can, and will, destroy the archaeological and historical sequence of an investigation. The metal detector, used correctly and responsibly, can and will aid the search if used to cover the spoil from a trench or to walk over a field, prior to the beginning of an excavation. In recent times, perhaps through televised archaeological programmes, the metal detector is reluctantly gaining a little respectability when employed responsibly and under supervision. Gradually breaking down the barrier of mistrust. Used responsibly, the metal detector is another tool to be employed.

Aviation archaeology is a relatively new phenomenon, similarly the aviation archaeologist. Like his traditional counterpart he, too, is a responsible investigator. It should be stressed that the aviation archaeologist has to procure a licence from the Ministry of Defence, as without this authorisation he, or anyone, excavating a crash site would be in breach of the law. The crashed aircraft is still the property of the Ministry of Defence, no matter how long ago the incident happened. Permission to proceed is not always granted, as the crash site may have military or other restrictions. The aviation archaeologist will have to provide a well researched case, prior to securing the necessary permission to proceed. This authorisation will allow him to legally excavate a crash site. He must also contact the appropriate local authorities to ensure that he is not in breach of any local covenants or restrictions.

There is a vast difference in the application of digging techniques when comparing the work of the aviation archaeologist to traditional methods applied by the conventional archaeologist. The former will, inevitably, have a metal detector lying beside his spade. A team will spend hours field-walking over the area, attempting to gain evidence from the geographical features, searching for unusual or unnatural evidence of what took place there. A gap in a line of trees, a depression in the ground, an area of vegetation which is different to the surrounding tract of land under investigation; their metal detectors traverse such anomalies as they proceed forward.

Long before the physical investigation proceeds, the recovery team will have spent many long and sometimes laborious hours examining the recorded evidence. Official documentation is painstakingly researched, local records examined, police reports scrutinized and any other avenue which might provide material answers is diligently examined. This includes a vital search for people who might have witnessed the incident or visited the site in the immediate aftermath of the event. It is regrettable that official records often raise as many questions as they answer. The exact location might be in question, the time recorded that the incident happened may vary considerably from document to document, witness to witness, likewise the recall of those involved. To navigate around these numerous pitfalls takes time and a great deal of patience. One such individual is Rick Penberthy. His heart is in World War II aviation archaeology, especially when RAF Warmwell is involved.

Far off the beaten track a stream meanders through a beautiful tranquil spot in the heart of Dorset's lush rural countryside. It was here that Sgt. Shepperd fought out the abrupt and dramatic last moments of his life.
Cooke.

Following similar paths of research, it was inevitable that Rick and the author would, at sometime in their research careers, get together. Often one of us would contact someone, only to find that the other had already been there. From this first meeting, a working relationship and personal friendship was formed that has endured for more years than either of us would care to remember. Rick's motives were to research the incidents, whereas the author's interest lay in researching RAF Warmwell's operational history, its squadrons and personnel. This mutual interest would become invaluable to both of us although we have diversified regarding our personal research projects. Over the years this has afforded us the privilege of forming personal friendships with some of the veterans and people who, as children, witnessed the events of those terrible years.

Rather than cover the numerous excavations that Rick has participated in, only two will be discussed, one in more detail than the other. His initial baptism into aviation archaeology began when a lady living in Wales contacted the incumbent at Holy Trinity Church, Warmwell, in an attempt to obtain information relating to the death of her brother, Sgt. P. Burrows, who died when his aircraft crashed near Frampton, Dorset. Rick and the author co-operated and were able to piece together the events of that April night in 1941. Sgt. Burrows flew as part of an abortive Bomber Command force attempting to destroy the German surface raiders, Scharnhorst and Gneisenau, sheltering under formidable defences around the harbour at Brest.

It is believed that this aircraft may have sustained damage from anti-aircraft fire whilst over the target. It is also understood that there was a mid-air collision involving a Wellington bomber, which was also participating in the operation. If this was the case, the machine that the Wellington collided with may have been the Blenheim that Sgt. Burrows was flying. If his aircraft was damaged and remained flyable, it would have taken all of the sergeant's skill to keep the machine airborne.

Sgt. Burrows was probably attempting to reach RAF Warmwell, although some accounts relate that he was attempting to reach another airfield. This has to be conjecture, as Warmwell would have been much closer and in his line of flight. Exactly what happened in the aircraft will never be known, but it seems certain that circumstances overtook the sergeant's valiant attempt to remain airborne, compelling him to attempt a forced landing in total darkness over invisible terrain.

Once committed to land, it was too late to abort the manoeuvre. The machine hit the ground with immense force and disintegrated, claiming the lives of all three crew members. The police report gave an indication of the horrific nature of the incident. It recorded that the aircraft was completely wrecked and at the time only Sgt. Burrows was positively identified, as his identity disc was recovered at the scene. It took a little longer to establish who the remaining crew members were. Of the three sergeants, only Sgt. Birdsell was buried at Holy Trinity, Warmwell. Sergeants Burrows and Perry were buried by their respective families.

Satisfied that he had examined all the known facts concerning the crash at Frampton, Rick was able to conclude his research and pass on what information he had gathered and any conclusions he had reached.

Almost immediately after the conclusion of this project, Rick received information about a crash site at Tadnol, not far from the former airfield. Initial research regarding combat losses during the Battle of Britain did not record the loss of an aircraft at this location. A search of police reports did reveal the date and time of the incident, recording that the aircraft was a Spitfire, but the report did not shed any light as to the possible cause of the incident. Additional research revealed that the Spitfire was R6607, assigned to 152 Squadron based at Warmwell. Rick was unable to find any further documentation relating to the cause of the crash, which tragically claimed the life of Sgt. Edmund Shepperd. A chance meeting led to Rick being introduced to a gentleman who had farmed the land during the war. He offered to show him where the Spitfire crashed, and led Rick across several fields. Finally, they reached a beautiful tranquil location, miles from habitation, amid lush farmland where a stream slowly meandered nearby.

Investigation and Recovery

Having established that the Spitfire was from 152 Squadron, Rick contacted the author to enquire if he had any information relating to the death of Sgt. Shepperd or the crash at Tadnol. The author was able to respond positively as he did have material regarding both the incident and Sgt Shepperd, also two of his close friends, but he would require time to search through his files. Meanwhile, Rick approached the present owner of the land who expressed great interest in his project and readily granted permission for him to further examine the crash site. A telephone call to experienced aviation archaeologist, John Cogram, brought reinforcements and on a cold autumn day John joined Rick, and Rick's children, James and Tessa, to brave a biting wind and lashing rain as they retraced

The repair plate dated 11-7-40 and damaged ammunition is laidover a photograph of pilots from 152 Squadron. Sgt. Shepperd is fourth from the left. The plate confirmed that R6607 had been repaired by Westland Aircraft at Yeovil with parts supplied by the Castle Bromwich Aeroplane Factory, Birmingham.
Cooke

Rick's previous trek. Painstakingly, under somewhat arduous conditions the group criss-crossed the fields in the area of the crash site but to no avail. Soaked to the skin and the light fading it was decided that, before calling it a day, they would briefly sweep along the wooded scrubland and marshy banks of the stream. Although it was not where Rick had been shown that the Spitfire crashed, almost immediately their metal detectors registered that something was buried beneath the surface. Carefully scraping away the grass and earth revealed a number of shattered .303 rounds. Subsequent examination of the remains of the cartridge cases showed that the ammunition was manufactured in the years 1938 and 1940.

Their enthusiasm boosted, it was decided to spread out and lengthen the search. In each direction that they walked, their detectors registered that beneath their feet there was something of a metallic nature. Hopefully, this would be more buried artefacts and not items of an agricultural nature. As the light was fading fast it was time to abandon the search for that day. Soaked to the skin but overjoyed that their day had proved positive, they returned to their cars and arranged a new date when they would return to closely examine what they hoped would be the remains of Spitfire R6607.

In subsequent visits, the site was examined much more closely. Interesting finds indicated that the Spitfire crashed with tremendous force and disintegrated on impact, spreading debris over a large area. Because of the marshy nature of the ground many of the fragments buried themselves into the soft earth and were not salvaged by the recovery team sent to retrieve the remains of the aircraft.

Fractionalised parts were identified from the fuselage, tail and wing sections and an important piece of evidence was the recovery of an identification plate, which enabled the team to finally prove that the aircraft was that flown by Sgt. Shepperd. The plate also revealed that R6607 had been repaired after a previous incident, which had occurred on 11 July 1940.

R6607

Rick and the team made a number of subsequent visits to the site returning, on each occasion, with more shattered remains of the Spitfire. As the aircraft had disintegrated over a substantial distance, most of the remains were not far below the surface, but R6607 was not going to yield all her secrets. In the immediate aftermath of the crash a recovery party was dispatched from Warmwell to retrieve and transport the remains of Sgt. Shepperd, his coffin draped in the Union Jack, to the airfield mortuary. A brief investigation of the incident began and a section of the CRU (Civilian Repair Unit) arrived to salvage the aircraft. This team removed the remains of the Spitfire to Cowley, where the aircraft was examined in an attempt to arrive at a conclusion as how or why it crashed. Any salvageable parts were dismantled, reconditioned and used to repair other damaged fighters. As will be appreciated, the original salvage operation removed vital material from the site. Rick, John Cogram and the team would have to base their findings on what remained at the site.

From the author's reference material, it was established that R6607 was one of a batch of 450 Spitfires supplied under contract No. 1971/39 at an initial contract price of £4,250 per machine. After delivery trials, R6607 served with four units prior to its transfer to 152 Squadron. During its tenure with No. 7 Operational Training Unit it sustained a Category 2 accident, resulting in a repair by Westland Aircraft. It was during this repair that the identification plate that enabled the team to establish which Spitfire they were investigating, was fitted. On 27 September 1940 the machine was transferred to 152

Squadron. Twenty-one days later it crashed at Tadnol, ending the career of a gifted pilot who almost certainly would have achieved 'Ace' status had he survived. One of the poignant final relics that the team unearthed emphasized the frailty of the human body and perhaps brought them close to Sgt. Shepperd. It was one of the magnets from the earphones fitted to his flying helmet!

Sgt. Shepperd

Over the weeks, Rick kept the author informed of their progress and invited him to view the crash site. Even on this occasion, R6607 continued to reveal further evidence of its fateful end beside what must be, in the height of summer, a beautiful tranquil spot. The author was also able to provide Rick with the background material he had promised, but he had to confess that he found the experience somewhat moving. His research over so many years brought him close to his subject and to the people who fought from RAF Warmwell.

Edmund "Dick" Shepperd was more than a name on a piece of paper. He was born at Binstead on the Isle of Wight in 1917 and tragically lost his father, who died of wounds he received in the Great War, two years after the birth of his son. An intelligent child, he dreamed of joining the RAF, an ambition which he achieved. After completing his initial training, he qualified as signals/wireless operator, and found himself posted to Egypt. Here he met two other signals types, Ralph Wolton and John Barker. The three formed a close friendship and, as war with Germany looked increasingly likely, the trio decided that they should apply for pilot training.

Returning to Britain and recently promoted to sergeants, the trio completed their training courses, gained their coveted 'Wings' and were posted to 152 Squadron at Acklington. Mundane convoy patrols and anti-invasions patrols proved boring in the extreme but gave the three pilots invaluable flying experience. To the south the early engagements of the Battle of Britain were being fought, but for 152 Squadron life tended to continue as though in peacetime, until early July 1940, when the squadron received orders to move to Warmwell. Sergeants Shepperd, Wolton and Barker were soon in the thick of the fighting defending the ports of Southampton, Portsmouth, Portland Harbour and the all-important radar sites. As the Battle grew in intensity, the Squadron flew east to defend London when requested by 11 Group Fighter Command.

Of the three pals, only Sergeant Wolton would survive the Battle of Britain and the war. Wounded in combat he returned to the squadron to learn that John Barker was lost over the Channel on 4 September. He and Sgt. Wolton both claimed two enemy aircraft destroyed whilst they served with 152 Squadron. By a quirk of fate it would be Dick Shepperd, whilst on leave at his home on the Isle of Wight, who witnessed his squadron's engagement with the enemy and confirmed Sgt. Wolton's claim for the destruction of a Junkers JU 88.

Shepperd, a popular man on the squadron, survived most of the hectic fighting of the Battle of Britain, claiming an Me 109 destroyed in the frenetic air battle to defend Warmwell when the station came under attack on 25 July. Three weeks later, on 12 August, he shot down a Junkers JU 88 bomber and six days later claimed the destruction of a Junkers JU 87 Stuka dive-bomber. The award of the Distinguished Flying Medal was usually granted when an NCO pilot shot down five or six enemy aircraft. The dispatch of a further JU 88 in the heavy autumn fighting over Dorset and Somerset on 7 October brought his tally to four. Had he survived, he almost certainly would have achieved this total, and more.

18 October 1940

Regrettably, controversy surrounds the loss of Sergeant Shepperd on 18 October. He was by now an experienced battle-hardened fighter pilot that the squadron could ill afford to lose. Scrambled in atrocious conditions to intercept an 'X Raid' (an unidentified plot on the radar), Shepperd led two other Spitfires into the gloom of low cloud and drifting rain. This worsened considerably as the flight searched in vain and followed various vectors designed to lead them to the unidentified aircraft. With no contact made they were finally instructed to return to base, but by now the weather had closed in and they were flying blind, cloud obscuring the ground. At some juncture the three Spitfires became separated.

Sergeant Shepperd knew he was nearing Warmwell but the conditions forced him to fly so low that he was 'hedge-hopping' just above the tree line, in an effort to locate his actual position. Although conjecture, when the author interviewed other pilots of the squadron, they expressed the same conclusions. These were that Shepperd almost certainly slid back his cockpit hood and raised his seat so that he could get a better view of the ground and, in all probability, he must have released his seat harness. Had he not done so, he might have survived the crash, but again, this is conjecture. What is certain is that R6607 clipped some trees, hit the ground and, disintegrating, careered through undergrowth, trees and bushes before the shattered remains came to rest in the small wooded area where Rick and his friends unearthed the remains of the aircraft.

The two remaining Spitfires made it back to Warmwell. Shepperd was overdue and radio transmissions to his aircraft remained unanswered. Meanwhile the squadron anxiously waited and hoped that he had landed safely somewhere and was making his way back to base. The wait was in vain; Sergeant Shepperd lay dead with the remains of his Spitfire. With all the aircraft on the station now grounded until further notice because of the weather, his squadron mates could not comprehend why the sortie had flown in such atrocious conditions.

Sergeant Edmund Shepperd was 33 at the time of his death and is buried near his Isle of Wight home of Binstead.

The Rubel Memorial

On 12 March 1944, Lt. Col. Clinton Wasem, Group Commander of the 474th Fighter Group assumed command of RAF Warmwell. The airfield's official designation was now Station 454, USAAF Moreton. Over the next few days and weeks, the Group (consisting of the 428th, 429th and 430th Fighter Squadrons) acclimatised itself to its new surroundings. It received its Lockheed P38 Lightning aircraft as it prepared to become operational, flying its first combat mission on 25 April.

Since becoming operational, the Group had flown various types of combat missions, including long-range bomber escort operations. Increasingly the Group was employed on fighter-bomber sorties in preparation for the imminent invasion of Europe. By 5 July, the operational record book of the 428th Fighter Squadron recorded the Group's 70th operational combat mission.

6 July 1944

The 474th Fighter Group, by this date, was frequently flying missions in support of ground operations. The first mission flown that day was a repeat of numerous other bombing and strafing missions. A supply dump was located and severely mauled. A convoy of over 25 vehicles was strafed and bombed, leaving numerous transport and armoured vehicles burning wrecks as the P38s reformed to return to base, where they arrived around 10:30 hours.

Later that day, at a little after 2pm, Col. Wasem, leading the HQ section, taxied out to take off and orbit the station. Meanwhile, Maj. Glass led the 429th into the air as the other squadrons formatted with those already airborne. The Group then turned south and flew out across the Channel.

The mission was a further armed recce to the Tours - Le Mans area. The operation called for the 430th Squadron to attack a separate target to its sister squadron - the 429th. 428th Squadron would divide its forces and provide fighter cover to the other squadrons, which were deployed as fighter-bombers. Two Flights would cover each squadron when the Group deployed near Tours. After the bombing attack had been completed the elements would reform and attack targets of opportunity on the withdrawal.

As they withdrew, the 429th strafed a number of ground targets but were initially intercepted by four Focke-Wulf 190 fighters. This encounter developed into a running fight as more FW190s joined the melee. The initial bounce claimed two P38s, which fell away in flames from an engagement that was gathering momentum. The estimate was that the P38s were engaging around twenty-five enemy aircraft. It was later confirmed that Lt. Robert Rubel and Lt. James Frederick from the 428th had become casualties, but it was not a totally one-sided affair. Pilots of the 429th had destroyed two enemy aircraft, claimed one as probably destroyed and three more as damaged. Lt. Banks hit his target so hard that, moments after the pilot baled out, the machine exploded in flames. Lt. Robert Milliken, who would later become one of only three pilots from the 474th Fighter Group to achieve 'ace' status, chased and shot down his first enemy aircraft.

Lt. Robert Rubel 474th Fighter Group. 2nd Lt. Robert J. Rubel 428 Squadron, 474th Fighter Group took off from Warmwell to participate on a Group combat mission from which he failed to return. He was killed in action on 6 July 1944.
Hanson/Hickok

Milliken's flight was forced to rapidly climb to ten thousand feet to defend the 428th, having seen one of the squadron's P38s being attacked by four FW190s.

Robert Milliken - *"I broke into a 190 coming in on our tail, but broke off as a 190 came in on me at about 5 o'clock. I racked to the right and in one turn was on the 190's tail, but after a deflection shot, lost him. Then I saw a 190 on the deck. He saw me and weaved to the left and right and must have chopped his throttle for I overshot him the first time. I closed to 175 yards and fired, and observed direct hits in the cockpit area. The pilot climbed out and his 'chute opened as he passed below me. The plane burst into flames and half-rolled into the ground."*

The action only lasted a few minutes – minutes, which would witness death and destruction. Seconds later the FW190s were withdrawing and soon were out of sight. The 474th regrouped and flew back to Warmwell.

The enemy fighters had attempted a classic attack - to dive on an unsuspecting enemy, hit him hard in one pass and withdraw, trying hard not to become embroiled in a sustained combat encounter. As the war progressed, the Allied air superiority often turned the balance in their favour but casualties were high on both sides.

Honouring Lt. Rubel - Montmerrie
6 July 2003

It was fifty-nine years to the day that the 474th had fought an engagement over the village of Montmerrie. The two P38s and FW190s lost that day crashed almost within sight of each other, the pall of smoke from each rising into the clear sky. Lt. Rubel's Lightning impacted the ground in a field approximately three quarters of a mile from the rural village where a small track dissected the road leading to the neighbouring village of Le Cerueil, four kilometres distant.

Jean-Claude Clouet, like many Frenchmen and women, pays homage to the memory of the men who helped to liberate France from the tyranny of Nazism. Much of his leisure time is spent researching and recovering the remains of crashed aircraft, honouring with dignity the memory of the pilots and ensuring that, wherever possible, memorials are placed in recognition of the sacrifice of a young life.

An example of his work was demonstrated when the author received a joint invitation from the Mayor of Montmerrie and Jean-Claude Clouet to attend an inauguration ceremony to honour Lt. Robert J. Rubel at the unveiling of a memorial dedicated to the pilot. The letter informed us that, accompanied by his son, Robert Milliken, a veteran of the 429th Fighter Squadron, would be in attendance - the sole participant involved in the wartime action who was able to make the trip from the USA.

The invitation came as a total surprise, followed two days later by a telephone call from Jean-Claude, requesting our presence at the inauguration ceremony. My wife, Carol, and I have the distinction of being honorary members of the 474th Fighter Group Association but at that moment I could not confirm whether we could make the trip, as it would literally have to be an overnight visit. Fortunately, we were able to make the necessary arrangements as the local newspaper was running offers on Ferry crossings and our son-in-law kindly volunteered to drive us. As he had satellite navigation in his car, we were confident that we would not get lost, as time was critical. The tickets were booked and we confirmed our acceptance to Jean-Claude. He, in turn, rang Robert Milliken to inform him of our attendance, so he was not surprised when I contacted him that evening.

Jean Claude Clouet.
Jean Claude Clouet, a principle member of the excavation team which recovered artefacts from the crash site where Lt. Rubel died, and from whom the author received an invitation to attend the ceremony to honour the pilot.
Carol Cooke

It was a warm, balmy July evening when we joined the queue for the overnight ferry to Cherbourg, where we landed at 6.30 the following morning. We then had a four hour drive to reach Montmerrie where the official ceremonies were due to commence at 10.30 a.m.

At the crossroads in the centre of the village we noticed, as we arrived, that a large crowd was gathering, including numerous standard bearers and a silver band. We drove on and parked near to the church where Mass was to be heard and a Service of Remembrance held. As we walked back along the road towards the assembled villagers, passers-by welcomed us.

Emerging from the crowd, Jean-Claude made us welcome and introduced us to Msr le Maire de Montmerrie, Norbert Hureau, members of the local council and other dignitaries. We met the local MP, Sylvia Bassot, Col. Jackson from the US Embassy in Paris and, the Guest of Honour, Robert Milliken. The silver band played marches and patriotic music as the congregation formed itself into a parade before the assemblage. Led by the band and standard bearing party we marched off towards the church of Notre-Dame-de-l'Assomption de Montmerrie for Mass and the Service of Remembrance. In the packed church, tributes were paid to Allied servicemen and women, Robert Milliken and Lt. Rubel. Prior to the conclusion of the service the band played a medley of music, which included the theme from the film 'The Longest Day'.

We had brought a poppy wreath with us, hoping that it might be laid during the inauguration ceremony. Jean-Claude asked the author to walk with him and Robert Milliken as the parade marched off toward the memorial, turning left at the crossroad. As we walked Bob Milliken talked of that day, fifty-nine years ago.

The local band leading the procession that marches to the inauguration of the memorial erected to honour Lt. Robert Rubel.
Terry Downton

We arrived at the Memorial to find it draped in the French Tricolour and the American flag. Further speeches were made in gratitude to those whose work led to the recovery of the P38 and who laboured to construct and erect the Memorial, and further tributes were paid to Lt. Rubel. The ceremony concluded with the laying of wreaths and further speeches made by various religious denominations. The congregation returned to reassemble at the Municipal Offices for a cheese and wine reception prior to departure to the neighbouring village of St-Christophe-la-Jajolet for a Remembrance Lunch which lasted three hours and included liberal glasses of calvados!

Regrettably, time was moving along all too fast. Jean-Claude invited us to join him as he took Bob Milliken to view the site where the FW190 he shot down, had crashed. Unfortunately, we had to decline in order to return to Cherbourg. Jean-Claude led us along the road toward the main highway, stopping at the site where a Sherman tank, assigned to a French regiment, had been knocked out in the fighting for the Falaise/ Argentan pocket, which witnessed the virtual destruction of the German army in France.

Having said our goodbyes we set off for Cherbourg, noticing signposts to the numerous cemeteries and many of the places that have become historically synonymous with the battle for Normandy. We had made good time and decided to make a short detour as we approached Bayeux, to visit the Commonwealth War Graves Cemetery. This is the largest cemetery in Normandy. 4,648 graves lie here, 3,935 of which are British. They stand sentinel to the slaughter of war; each a son, a husband or brother. It is a very moving, solemn place.

IN MEMORY OF
2nd LIEUTENANT O-758074
✡
ROBERT J. RUBEL
PILOTE

428th FS 9 474th FG

U·S·A·A·F

MORT POUR NOTRE LIBERTÉ
LE 6-07-44
LE 6·07·2003   Nº 64 HN

The memorial inscription to Lt. Robert Rubel, inaugurated 59 years after his death just outside of the village of Montmerrie in Normandy.
Cooke

Robert Milliken.
The author and Robert C. Milliken (left) who flew on the mission when Lt. Rubel was killed; travelled from the USA to honour his comrade and attend the memorial dedication.
Terry Downton

The next morning we left our hotel and drove to the harbour area of Cherbourg and wandered around the inner harbour. Above us, overlooking the harbour, is the fortress that cost American forces dear. To capture Cherbourg the Americans paid the price of over 22,000 casualties. We walked around the inner harbour where, in October and November 1943 Whirlwinds of 263 Squadron based at Warmwell, attacked the German freighter, the Munsterland, sheltering beneath Cherbourg's formidable anti-aircraft defences. Our visit was over and at 10:30 we joined the queue of vehicles to return home.

On occasions, aviation archaeology is controversial but, on the whole, the vast majority of people involved in the research and excavation of crashed wartime aircraft do so honourably, often answering outstanding questions which official records have left incomplete. Through their work, surviving relatives have, in some cases, been able to witness their relations being given a last resting place and burial with full military honours.

Tank.
Across Normandy are numerous memorials dedicated to the ferocious fighting to liberate France. None more tangible than this French crewed Sherman tank which stands where it was knocked out by a single round in the desperate fighting around Falaise.
Terry Downton

Cherbourg inner harbour.
The harbour at Cherbourg. It was here that the Whirlwinds of 263 Squadron attacked the German blockade runner the Munsterland.
Cooke

Ivan Mason

For such men as Rick and Jean-Claude, there will always be questions. Occasionally the answers cannot be found in official documentation or from the archaeological remains. The anecdotal research compiled by an historian is needed.

Many years ago, I had written a piece, which I signed off as "An RAF Warmwell Historian" only to receive a challenge to the word 'historian'. How does one class what an historian is? Is he an author who writes about his subject; one who spends much of one's time researching a subject, purely for his or her own satisfaction? Does he or she require academic qualifications? Almost certainly, it is an open-ended question and I leave it to the reader to arrive at their own conclusions. It would be a grave error not to include a man in this section, who has spent much of his life researching and recording Warmwell's past. He is Ivan Mason.

Ivan is a modest man but one who has lived life to the full. A retired teacher, in his younger days, after National Service he enlisted and spent nineteen years in the Royal Air Force Volunteer Reserve. He retained a love for the sea and, when time permitted, he sailed. However he never lost his interest in aviation and found time in his busy schedule to become a part time journalist. Writing on a variety of subjects, often wartime matters and on the subject of RAF Warmwell when the opportunity arose. He is also the author of some very interesting books. To me, Ivan's pinnacle of achievement is that he has the distinction of being the author of the RAF Warmwell section of the massive tome - The Battle of Britain Then and Now.

Our individual research careers often followed similar courses; meeting the same people, arriving to interview someone only to learn that one or the other of us had already been there first, or to be advised to contact this other chap. Inevitably we met, 'hit if off' immediately, and have remained good friends ever since. In 1984 we had the honour of working together, to assist the late Bob Hanson and his wife, Marilyn. They were arranging for veterans of the 474th Fighter Group Association to return to the European bases from which they flew during the war, including Warmwell, which held a great significance for Bob.

Sadly, Robert Hanson passed away but he had set in motion a healthy movement of veterans. Marilyn continued to work within the Association and later married Gene Hickok, a former pilot in the Group, who had also flown from Warmwell. Together they began planning a further trip to Europe and, again, Ivan and I volunteered our services. In 1994, the 474th Fighter Group Association returned to the U.K. and friends were once more united.

Over the years, Ivan's files bulged. Many hours were spent at the Public Records Office at Kew, and at local centres. Hundreds of books were read, their pages scanned for the briefest mention of Warmwell or the squadrons that served there. Numerous veterans were traced and their anecdotes and stories recorded, but when Ivan decided to retire from his research projects (if one ever does!) he generously passed to the author his vast archive of Warmwell material.

Ivan's work laid the foundation stone for those of us who have followed in his footsteps and continue to add to the vast pool of knowledge which he began to compile more years ago than either of us would probably care to remember.

Profile of a Battle of Britain Pilot: Ralph Wolton

On a ship returning to the UK in 1938, three men *"All signals types"* to quote Ralph Wolton, formed a close friendship. This was a bond that would endure throughout the summer fighting of 1940, although only one of the pals would survive the Battle of Britain and, ultimately, the war.

Edmund Eric Shepperd, John Barker and Ralph 'Bob' Wolton had volunteered for pilot training. Their applications were successful and they left Egypt on board a ship bound for England. When their training was completed and they had gained their coveted 'Wings', the trio were posted to 152 Squadron. The Squadron was being formed at Acklington under the tutelage and command of Squadron Leader Peter Devitt. In reality, the squadron had been established initially on 1 June 1918 at Rochford, as a Sopwith Camel night-fighter unit. They moved to France in mid-October but the war ended three weeks after their arrival. A little over seven months later, on 30 June 1919, the squadron was disbanded.

It was re-formed on 1 October 1939 and equipped with Gloster Gladiators, becoming operational during the first week of November. In January of the new year, the squadron received its first Spitfire. Over the coming weeks, more Spitfires would be received but the squadron's ageing Gladiators were retained for night flying duties. The Spitfire's narrow undercarriage, glare from the exhaust and difficult forward vision when taxiing led to landing mishaps in the darkness. During the day, Spitfires were utilized for the laborious task of convoy, shipping and coastal patrols. One boring day followed another and the Squadron existed on a more-or-less peacetime basis in the relative quiet of northern Britain. When the order to move south was received, many of the pilots were on leave, including Ralph Wolton. He received a telegram instructing him to report to the squadron at RAF Warmwell. The advance party had left Acklington on 10 July 1940; the unit packed and completed the transition south by 12 July. By this date the squadron had totally relinquished its Gladiators and was wholly equipped with Spitfires.

"At Acklington" Wolton commented *"We could sense that the full force of war was not far away. The winter had been too peaceful."* This was the time known historically as the Phoney War. All too soon, 152 Squadron would be in the thick of the fighting, defending south-western England, Southampton, Portsmouth and the vital Naval installations and harbour at Portland and flying east to defend London when requested by 11 Group, Fighter Command.

Warmwell, a training and gunnery station, became a forward airbase in early July since the arrival of fighter squadrons at the sector HQ airfield of Middle Wallop. It would take a few days for 152 Squadron to become fully operational. It *"immediately went about the job of settling in and getting to know its way around the new station"*. Accommodation was scarce, airmen were already being billeted off the station, but billets were found for the unit as alerts and scrambles became commonplace. The airfield's location offered a grandstand view of the Luftwaffe's raids on Portland Harbour.

On 19 July, the squadron flew its first operational sortie, and the next day suffered its first war casualty when one officer failed to return from combat off the Isle of Wight. A few days later, the squadron would avenge that loss of P/O Posner, a South African volunteer. This day would be Bob Wolton's combat initiation. *"Led by S/L Devitt, the full squadron was scrambled on 25th July."* Climbing hard, the squadron passed over Portland – the enemy formation ahead of them. *"Our earphones crackled with excited voices as we spotted the enemy. Leading us in, the C.O. called 'Tally Ho' over the R/T to inform the Controller that we were about to attack. My earphones were suddenly alive with the chatter of battle, both British and German."*

The reason that Wolton could hear German transmissions was that the frequency used by them was very close to that used by the RAF. Moments later the squadron clashed with the enemy formation. *"P/O 'Ferdinand' Holmes led the section to which I was assigned. Holmes banked and made his pass at the Hun aircraft and seconds later I followed him in. The Dornier came into my gunsight and I pressed the firing button and watched my tracer ammunition strike home."* Although he knew he had hit the enemy aircraft in an encounter that had lasted only seconds, Sgt Wolton noted that *"There were no outward signs that it had caused any real damage."*

Pulling away from the combat he found himself to the south of a small group of Junkers JU 87 Stuka dive-bombers, *"– apparently unmolested by our unit or any other. So I made a banking turn and began my pursuit of them."* Thinking that the dive-bombers were about to attack their target, he closed in rapidly upon them. *"My diving attack caused them to scatter and I latched on to one of their number and fired the remainder of my ammunition at him."* Smoke began to trail from the JU 87 which, moments later, went into a steep dive. Bob Wolton then made the cardinal error, which must have cost many fighter pilots their lives. Luckily there were no enemy fighters able to reach him before he realised the error of his ways. He opened the throttle. *"I followed hard after it. I suddenly realised this was a foolish thing to do, so I immediately pulled out and began to take evasive action in case I became the prey of one of the Me109's giving the slower Stukas fighter cover. The last I saw of the JU 87, it was still diving toward the English Channel."*

As so often happened, the sky was devoid of aircraft. Fighter pilots frequently comment on this phenomenon. One moment the sky is full of aircraft locked in combat and seconds later one is alone in a seemingly vacant sky. Sgt Wolton made for base, keeping an ever-watchful eye on his rear-view mirror.

Sgt. Wolton was the second man in a section of three aircraft led by Holmes; the third member, F/O Christopher 'Jumbo' Deanesly was missing. After attacking the Dornier he also went for the Stukas. Return fire hit his Spitfire and, wounded, he ditched into the sea. He was rescued and spent time in hospital before returning to duty.

Bob Wolton recalls *"Later that day we received the news that at least two JU 87's were seen to fall into the sea and that the Dornier our section attacked, had crashed near Weymouth, killing one of its crew."* Wolton would share the claim for the Dornier, which crashed near the brickworks at Chickerell. It featured in many newspapers at the time and subsequent post war books; and he was granted a 'kill' for one of the JU 87's.

Life for the squadron, and those units from Middle Wallop which operated from Warmwell as a forward airbase, became exceedingly hectic. Scramble after scramble sent them off three, four and occasionally fives times a day. Section and flight scrambles were commonplace, and not infrequently the full squadron was ordered up. H.Q. would estimate the danger from the radar plot and execute a scramble to combat whatever strength it determined the threat to be. Quite often, a pair of machines would race off, soon followed by the remainder of the Flight. Sgt. Walton had to wait until 15 August to engage the enemy again. On this occasion he faced an Me110 head on, attacked some JU 87s and needed to dig deep into his personal resolve, hold his nerve and remain calm in a situation of absolute adversity. Too low to use his parachute, he had to extricate himself from his Spitfire while plunging towards the sea. So deep in the water that there was no light above him to reveal the surface, he had to take control of his fear and allow himself to begin to float toward the surface, before kicking out. As with a later equally harrowing escape Sgt. Wolton's self control saved his life where many men would have lost their resolve to survive.

10 Group, alerted to a threatening raid developing across the Channel, brought the whole squadron to 'a state of readiness'. Minutes later it was airborne and vectored toward the incoming raid approaching Portland. It comprised of Junkers 87 dive-bombers escorted by Messerschmitt 109 and Me110 fighters. Sgt. Wolton remembers: *"Sections of the squadron went for the dive-bombers while the rest of us attacked the covering fighters. Turning, I faced an Me110."* The Spitfire and Messerschmitt rapidly closed upon each other. Moments later, the twin-engined enemy fighter filled his gun sight. *"We closed on each other at a combined speed of well over 500 mph, and, when in range, I fired at him. His tracer flew toward and around me, then he seemed to swerve away and both of us took evasive action."* As the fighter sped past him, Sgt. Wolton could not determine if he had hit the machine. Passing so close, he could see where oil stains streamed along the underside of the aircraft.

To the west, in Lyme Bay, he observed some Stukas diving to attack a ship. Opening the throttle, he raced in pursuit, and stormed into the dive-bombers, causing them to scatter. He noted that *"return fire arched toward me but with no effect."*

His attack on the JU 87s had been at speed. Pulling up, he began to climb as rapidly as he could, but at this moment he was very vulnerable. He was flying UM-F. *"F for Freddie suddenly shook and vibrated. There followed instantaneously, two explosions and gaping holes appeared in the wings. The cockpit immediately began to fill with fumes and a check of the instruments revealed the water temperature was going off the gauge."* Reaching out, he shut down the engine, probably moments before it seized up. As so often happened, Wolton had not seen his attacker, although experience had taught him to keep an ever-watchful eye on the rear-view mirror. After being the hunter, he had fallen prey to one of the protecting fighter screen. His situation was desperate and there was no alternative but to evacuate the aircraft. The action of sliding back the canopy caused an inrush of air, clearing the glycol fumes, which had consumed the interior of the cockpit. His vision now returned and he was surprised to find that he was alone in an empty sky. He observed that *"the Chesil Bank seemed only about a mile away. Rather than bale out I decided to glide to a landing."* The damage sustained by UM-F had not caused the aircraft to catch fire. Such were the Spitfire's flying characteristics Bob decided that, from this height and position, reaching the shore line should not prove too difficult. Wolton's returning confidence was, however, suddenly and violently shattered. *"The aircraft dropped its nose and went into a vertical dive"* he recalled. Gravity gripped the fighter and it plummeted headlong toward the sea, out of control. Trapped in his cockpit as he fought to regain some control over the plunging aircraft, his situation was now desperate. He had to extract himself from the Spitfire or remain with it as it descended into the depths of the Channel. At some point he had released his seat harness but he had no actual recall of when he had done this. His imminent death must have become a stark reality in those terrifying moments. Fortunately, in this moment of despair, fate or luck played its part *"Somehow or another, I managed to invert the aircraft and must have dropped from the cockpit shortly before it hit the water."* Whether it was fate or just his will to survive,

Wolton's modesty would not allow himself to be drawn further regarding his miraculous escape.

Ralph Wolton has no further recall as to what actually happened in the moments after he fell from the fighter. He believed that he was probably knocked unconscious as he fell out of the Spitfire or when he hit the sea. His next terrifying conscious recollection is *"regaining consciousness and not being able to breathe. Everything around me was dark and freezing cold."* He had plunged countless feet beneath the sea, yet somehow this man was able to control his fear and hold what little remained of his breath. Rising from the depths he swam toward the lightening surface of the water.

He was an exceptionally strong swimmer. The time spent fighting to reach the surface must have seemed like an eternity. Finally he broke the surface, coughing and gasping for air. *"My lungs ached and I felt deeply sick"*, he recalled. *"I had released my parachute harness, how or when I did this I do not know but I managed with great difficulty to inflate my Mae-West."* Self-inflating lifejackets were to come later in the war, for Battle of Britain pilots shot down over the sea, it was necessary to either partially inflate the life jacket before take off which inhibited movement within the cockpit or "huff and puff" into the tube while drifting on one's parachute. For those who could not swim or were unable to inflate their life preserver, the descent, facing almost certain drowning, must have been agonising.

Sgt. Wolton released the bag of fluorascene, which turned the sea around him a bright green colour. This would enable a searching aircraft to find a downed pilot in the sea. The spotter aircraft would inform the controller and, hopefully, a naval craft or a launch from the marine craft unit at Lyme Regis would be dispatched to the rescue.

Injured, Bob Wolton had further hurdles to overcome as he regained some of his composure and he began to check himself over. *My shoes were missing, as were my wrist watch and flying helmet."* He recalled that *"My legs, although beginning to go numb due to exposure to the cold water, began to ache. I found that my ankle had sustained a severe cut, this being the cause of the pain."* Wolton's position was becoming precarious. Exposure and shock were already taking hold and his quick rescue was vital if he was to survive.

In the distance, he could see the shore and decided he could swim to the Chesil Bank. Moored much closer was a floating target raft, used by the gunnery and bombing schools operating from Warmwell. Forcing himself on, he swam toward the raft and, with great difficulty, hauled himself aboard it. The trauma and exertion exhausted him and *"As I climbed from the sea I became violently sick from the large amount of sea water I had swallowed and inhaled."* He decided to rest for a while before continuing his endeavour to reach the shore. As he lay there on the raft, he heard the sound of powerful engines in the distance. Its bow raised and creaming the sea, one of the launches from the 37MCU, the Lyme Regis based marine craft unit, powered toward him at a rate of knots. Moments later the launch was alongside the raft. *"Firm hands grabbed me and I was lifted onto the boat, where my ankle received attention as the launch raced towards its base. Soon I was on dry land and in hospital. Here I would stay for the next two weeks, after which I had a short spell of leave."*

Ralph Wolton spent his leave with his mother and wrote of his return to the squadron. *"When I returned to Warmwell a shock awaited me."* His friend Sgt. John Barker, with whom he and Eric 'Dick' Shepperd had returned to the UK to begin their flying training, was missing in action. *"The squadron had been engaged in some heavy fighting."* he related *"I learnt that John was missing after a fight on 4 September. He, like myself and Sgt. Dick Shepperd, had all returned to the UK together to begin a pilots' course shortly before war broke out. They, like myself, had been signals personnel and our careers had followed parallel paths. Of the three, I was the only one to survive 1940. Dick died a few weeks after my return, in a flying accident."* (Details of Sgt. Shepperd's death are related elsewhere in this volume.)

The loss of his friends made a profound impression on Bob Wolton. Sgt. Albert Kearsey of 152 Squadron confessed to the author, that as the Battle progressed and pals were lost, the old hands made the conscious decision not to become too friendly with the new recruits who were posted to the squadron, remaining somewhat aloof and detached. As Sgt. Kearsey related, *"New faces arrived one day and seemed to go missing the next."* Bob Wolton and other pilots felt the same. Their fighting was hard and so was their play. Often burning the candle at both ends, they would return to the airfield in the small hours, sleeping off the night's rigours at the dispersal. Before dawn they would be at 'readiness', awaiting the Luftwaffe.

Following his return to duty after his hospitalisation, Ralph Wolton's life became a hectic turmoil of combat flying, frequently engaging the enemy. *"The Battle was on in earnest"* he recalled. *"We were sent up on many occasions, often it was just a section or flight. On 25 September the whole squadron was ordered aloft to engage a large formation of bombers making for Bristol."* The fight was long and hard and vapour trails criss-crossed the sky. High above them the people of Dorset and Somerset witnessed the drama unfold, although by now such occasions were becoming commonplace. Sgt Wolton: *"The sky seemed full of aircraft, some of our fighters going for the bombers and others engaging the swarms of Me109s and Me 110s. I was involved in a number of attacks but although I must have hit some of my targets, nothing went down to my knowledge."* The squadron lost two more pilots, whom it could hardly afford to lose.

The next day Sgt. Wolton was again in action, flying as No. 2 to F/L Derek Boitel-Gill, one of 152 Squadron's most capable and deadly pilots. Boitel-Gill's tally of 'kills' was growing steadily and, on this occasion, he was leading the squadron. By the end of the Battle of Britain, Boitel-Gill would have shot down eight enemy aircraft and claim a share in another, and almost certainly must have contributed to the destruction of others. Regrettably, he lost his life in a flying accident early in the following year, after gaining promotion to the rank of Wing Commander.

Bob Wolton: *"Boitel-Gill led our section toward the Isle of Wight, climbing to gain the advantage. Over the R/T the controller informed our leader that the enemy were entering our area, and seconds later Boitel-Gill's voice calmly announced that he had spotted a formation of JU 88s to the south and above us."* The enemy formation had the advantage at that moment but Boitel-Gill's tactics were equal to the situation. He ordered the squadron into a line astern formation, and then took them into a steep power dive before climbing hard, in an effort to gain both height and speed when they smashed into the enemy. *"In line astern we went into a steep dive to gain speed then, pulling the stick back, we climbed hard. To my surprise the Junkers seemed unaware of our approach and made no attempt to take any evasive action. Roaring into the formation from below, we took them entirely by surprise."* Within seconds, three of them had fallen.

Sgt. Wolton engaged a number of targets in the hectic mêlée of Spitfires and enemy bombers, one of which he damaged so severely that it immediately began to fall away and dropped toward the sea. *"I fired at several aircraft"* he related *"one of which began to fall."*

Watching the engagement from the cliffs near his Binstead home on the Isle of Wight was Dick Shepperd. He confirmed Sgt. Wolton's claim for the destruction of one of the Junkers JU 88s. *"Witnessing this combat was my good friend Dick Shepperd; he was on leave and watched the action from the cliffs near his home."* Wolton related. On his return to Warmwell Wolton reported to the squadron intelligence officer and submitted his combat report, but he had to wait some days before his claim was verified and granted.

September for 152 Squadron proved to be a hectic month, as it was for all the Middle Wallop sector squadrons. They were not only covering their own territory but flying east to reinforce II Group units when requested. Combat encounters were plentiful and, although these did not always involve the whole squadron, nevertheless casualties mounted. Bob Wolton, like so many in Fighter Command, was living on his nerves. Lack of sleep and food were a constant problem, the squadron often being airborne at mealtimes. He related *"Our staple diet was one of hurried cakes, sandwiches and tea, all grabbed as we waited between scrambles. The mobile tea van which visited the dispersal was a Godsend."*

All of Warmwell's pilots and ground crews regarded the tea van as their saviour in a time of dire need. One arrived from the Salvation Army and a more frequent one was driven by a young girl, escorted by a lady on a large white horse. Just as important was the need to get away from the airfield and the rigours of their daily routine. The queue was frequently long as numerous young lads waited for the Liberty Bus. Often the pilots would cram themselves into someone's car, dangerously overloading it, and roar off to 'cut up' the bus making its sedate way to Dorchester or Weymouth. Once deposited at the venue of their choice, a riotous sojourn ensued. More often that not, the local constabulary turned a blind eye to the youthful skylarking that followed. *"Our dispersal was littered with our trophies"* Bob recalled *"Road signs, hat stands, toilet seats, the items soon mounted up. Every so often the local police would arrive and collect them. The C.O. would give us all another lecture about not bringing things back, then the whole process would begin again."*

By early October the warmth of the late summer breeze gave way to a chill in the morning air and the green of summer surrendering to a landscape of ochre, but the squadrons were still fighting for survival and October would witness some vicious and hotly contested actions over the southwest. October 7 was a day of particularly violent and frenzied activity. 152 Squadron sustained a further loss when recently promoted P/O Akroyd crashed near Wynford Eagle. He was taken to Dorset County Hospital, where he succumbed to his injuries. 609 Squadron lost Sgt. Feary, who baled out too low for his parachute to deploy. To the squadrons there appeared to be no respite, and on 11 October Ralph Wolton once more found his courage tested to the extreme.

The whole squadron was scrambled and ordered to patrol over Dorchester. Bob Wolton related what followed to the author, again his modesty devaluing his trial over adversity. He was totally conscious throughout and must have had time to contemplate his fate, were he not able to release his parachute. He fell, without restraint, some 12 – 13,000 feet. Such was the haste to get airborne that he was not fully clothed, wearing only his pyjamas, flying jacket and boots. In his haste, he had not had time to lock and fasten his Sutton harness seat restraint or secure his parachute about himself. He had only slipped his arms though the upper straps and slid the parachute beneath him prior to take-off. He found himself in mid-air and falling; his parachute, unattached to his lower torso, streamed out above him. How does one fall that distance, remaining calm, pulling the parachute to oneself and holding it securely enough to pull the rip-cord? My words cannot do justice to the danger of Bob's predicament or his courage. His words are modest in the extreme!

"I was tail-end Charlie, whose job it was to protect the formation from attack from the rear. My aircraft needed to be jinked and darted about keeping vigil. Suddenly, without warning, the squadron dived away. Caught unawares I pushed the stick forward, opened the throttle and dived after them. I was diving very hard, when my aircraft began to vibrate violently. There quickly followed a terrific crunch as one of the wings began to detach itself."

His Spitfire was minus a wing, totally uncontrollable and beginning to break up, gyrating forces plummeting it earthwards. It all happened so suddenly that he probably did not have time to realized what was actually happening. Literally catapulted out of the cockpit, he was falling. *"I reached for the rip-cord, but it was not where it should have been. I realised that I had not secured my parachute as I took off* (and) *began searching for it frantically and then I heard the voice of my old instructor saying – Don't fumble, look for the damned thing!."*

"I searched again for my parachute, which was trailing away from me wrapped around one of my arms. Pulling it to me I was able to bring the parachute close enough to hang on to both straps. Finding the rip-cord, I tugged at it, to my immense relief the parachute billowed out above me. I must have fallen about 13,000 feet, my parachute saving me at only 1,200 feet."

"I landed on the lawn of a farmhouse just outside Dorchester. Apart from a few scratches on my legs I was none the worse for wear. My Spitfire crashed nose first into the ground near the farmhouse. (The wing came down over a mile and a half away, on the other side of a wooded hill. Author) *Within minutes I was taken to the house and from there to a military hospital at Kingston Maurward for a check up, returning to the squadron a few hours later."*

The autumnal weather was gradually deteriorating as the Luftwaffe diversified its tactics, gradually relinquishing the predominance of daylight bombing raids and sending frequent fighter incursions over the southwest. At night, London and other major cities resounded to the sound of throbbing engines, screaming bombs and shattering explosions. Southern counties continued to witness numerous hard fought engagements. Gradually combat encounters decreased, noticeably in the final two weeks of the month.

It was during October that his other close friend, Eric Shepperd, died in what most of the squadron's personnel felt was an unnecessary scramble. In atrocious weather conditions he chased an unconfirmed plot on the radar. Sgt. Wolton: *"Dick Shepperd and another pilot were sent up in rather heavy cloud to intercept a lone plane. They never saw it and they lost sight of each other. The circumstances of his death indicated that Dick was trying to identify his position and had probably tried to get below the cloud base. He crashed into a hill just six miles from the airfield."*

By November, the Battle of Britain was almost fought to its conclusion. Combat encounters were only happening once or twice a week, often with no conclusion, although a pronounced action was fought off the Isle of Wight on 28 November, when 152 lost two pilots in an engagement with fighters from JG2. 609 Squadron also suffered two casualties in the fight, one of these was F/L Dundas, a squadron 'ace'. He has been credited with shooting down Geshwaderkommodore Helmut Wieck, at that time revered as the highest scoring Luftwaffe pilot. Unfortunately, neither side could produce a witness to confirm who the victor was over the Geshwaderkommodore.

As for Sgt. Wolton, he had survived and was long overdue a 'rest' from operational flying. On 16 November he received orders to report to a new posting, at a flying training unit, to qualify as an instructor. In this capacity, he would train both British and American pilots in the U.K. He flew his final operational sortie with 152 Squadron on 5 December. *"I led a section of three Spitfires to intercept an enemy aircraft. We never saw it and then, due to bad weather, we became separated as we returned to the airfield. We all landed safely however."*

Of the three friends who departed from North Africa, only Ralph Wolton survived. Whilst being trained to become an instructor he fell into conversation with a wing commander. Coincidentally, this officer had investigated the crash of 11 September and had concluded that the crash was due to structural failure. The radiator had been incorrectly fitted, either during manufacture or during a major service. Bob Wolton related: *"The force exerted on the wing caused the bolts holding the glycol radiator to strip from their mounting and the radiator to detach itself, which in turn caused the starboard wing to disintegrate."*

Later in the war, Bob Wolton was posted to 100 Group and flew Mosquitoes on counter-radio operations in support of Bomber operations. He retired from the RAF as Flight Lieutenant in 1948. Sadly this man of exceptional nerve and courage is no longer with us but his life was never without an element of danger and excitement. A life-long motorcycle enthusiast, he entered the trade and competed in circuit racing, including a number of TT races on the Isle of Man. He then owned his own light engineering business, retaining his love of motorcycles into retirement, when he attended the regular meetings of a club near his home in Somerset.

I met Bob Wolton for the last time in 1988. He had driven to Yeovilton to meet my wife and I at the RNAS Air Day, where members of the Memorial Committee were raising funds for a memorial stone to honour those who fought at Warmwell. As we sat and drank coffee, I asked him how he felt about having a memorial erected to honour Warmwell's contribution to victory in World War Two. He said, with a grin on his face *"Old – very old!"* I make no apology for being in awe of this man, not tall in stature but huge in courage! Not that Bob would agree with my conclusion, his modesty would not permit this.

Ralph Wolton is just one of many young men who rose to the challenge of defending this country when its back was against the wall. Historians rightly concluded that had 'The Few' not won the Battle, Britain would most likely have had to sue for peace. 'The Few' bought the opportunity for Britain to fight on, with their courage and their lives.

RAF Warmwell Memorial Appeal

Like Warmwell, numerous airfields were constructed in the immediate pre-war period and many more as the war progressed, including several along the southern coast of Britain. All did sterling work but were frequently overshadowed by their more famous sisters. Warmwell is one such airfield – a Battle of Britain fighter station. Its location in 10 Group did not give the airfield the exposure that stations within 11 and 12 Group received, yet for almost five years its squadrons flew from the grass flying field to engage the enemy. Situated a few minutes' flying time from the coast, it nestled in the tranquillity of Dorset's rolling hills and heathland, deep in the heart of Thomas Hardy country.

The threat of attack was never far away from the thoughts of those who maintained the aircraft and the station; those on the ground accepted but never fully came to terms that Warmwell was, and frequently did, become a target of the Luftwaffe. Today few people have heard of it, or the pivotal role it played throughout Britain's darkest hours.

Warmwell has often featured in the local press; sometimes the statements printed have been erroneous, which has brought a response from local historians and archaeologists who have worked for many years to record Warmwell's history and write of the sterling deeds achieved there. It was in reply to an article in the press in 1987 that one historian wrote lengthy letters to explain Warmwell's role and that he thought it was time that Warmwell's history was commemorated with a memorial and, more importantly, dedicated to the men and women who fought from there.

A frequent contributor to a local newspaper joined the debate, which motivated some members of the Wool Branch of the Royal Air Forces Association and various members of the public to form a committee for that express purpose, assembling for its inaugural meeting late in that year and publishing its "Declaration of Intent" in January 1988. From that moment the committee worked tirelessly to raise funds for a memorial stone to be raised on or near the airfield site. A travelling photographic exhibition was compiled from the archives of one of its members. This was taken to the Great Dorset Steam Fair, a number of air displays and numerous village fetes. Meanwhile, bookmarkers, pens and saleable items marked with the RAF Warmwell Memorial Appeal's logo were marketed.

The committee published its quest and appealed for donations and notable with their benevolence were ECC Quarries Ltd and ARC Ltd; the local managers of the quarries passing their entire charity budget for that year to the appeal. Ex-Warmwell veterans donated generously, as did the general public and commercial companies, which allowed the appeal committee to set a provisional date for the dedication. During this period Crossways Parish Council approached the committee and offered the present site provided permission could be obtained from the construction company who was developing a housing estate on the former airfield and from previous landowners, each of whom had placed codicils on the land. They, too, were immediate in giving their blessing to the project. Meanwhile a stone mason and reunion advisor and other members were co-opted to the committee. Finally the Appeal Committee were able to publish the date of the dedication – 10/11 June 1989.

Planning permission was granted and as the date grew closer work began on the erection of a Purbeck Stone memorial and the erection of a pair of iron gates depicting two fighter aircraft, made by apprentices of the UKAEE Winfrith; meanwhile plans were executed to stage a reunion of Warmwell veterans, to which members of the general public were invited, especially those people who had so generously donated toward the appeal.

Over the weekend of 10/11 June all the planning came to fruition and a most successful reunion was held at Warmwell Leisure Centre, reuniting many old friends from those far off years.

On the afternoon of Sunday 11 June the memorial to RAF Warmwell was dedicated at a public ceremony, a band travelled from Oxford to entertain those present followed by a Service of Dedication, during which the memorial was unveiled by a Warmwell veteran who had served on the Appeal Committee. Finally, an address was given by a pilot who flew with 152 Squadron during its attachment to the airfield.

Since its dedication the Memorial has become the focal point of Remembrance each year as Crossways honours those who gave their lives whilst stationed at RAF Warmwell, and has seen the return of many veterans including members of the USAAF.

On 4 June 1994 the 474th Fighter Group Association made a second pilgrimage to Dorset as veterans, their wives and relations visited the European bases from which the Group flew. Ivan Mason (who wrote the Warmwell section of the Battle of Britain Then and Now) and the author had worked closely with the veterans and at their behest had arranged a Service of Remembrance and Dinner. Association President, Ralph Embrey, poignantly stood before the Memorial and in a moving ceremony laid a wreath to pay homage to comrades who lost their lives whilst flying with the Group from the airfield. Continuing the theme of Remembrance, Crossways held further ceremonies and staged a very successful photographic exhibition and display of Warmwell memorabilia. Later that evening at a

Cooke

Bournemouth hotel, the veterans held a Dinner of Remembrance, attended by the Mayor of Bournemouth, dignitaries from Crossways and Dorchester, and friends whom they had met on the first visit in 1984. During the after-dinner speeches three oil paintings depicting a Lockheed P.38 Lightnings from the 428th, 429th and 430th squadrons which the Group comprised of, were presented to the Group Association and in an almost tearful reunion former pilot, Col. William Chickering was reunited with 'Down & Go' – the aircraft he flew as a young Lieutenant, albeit on canvas. Shortly after, amid fond farewells, the veterans departed to travel on the overnight ferry to France where they were to officially participate in the events to commemorate the D Day landings.

A number of displays and fund raising exhibitions have been staged and these events have enabled Crossways Parish Council to donate the proceeds to the Royal Air Forces Benevolent Fund, thereby honouring the airfield and its personnel, and maintaining a peacetime extension of Warmwell's past and hopefully bringing the deeds and experiences of a foregone generation to those of today.

Crossways Parish Council. Chairman's Badge of Office.
Hann

I'll Never Forget Her

Perhaps the final word can be left to the late Bob Hanson, a former pilot of the 474th Fighter Group who was instrumental in the formation of the Veterans' Association. During the 1984 visit he was asked by the author what his recollections of Warmwell were. He replied, with emotion in his voice "Warmwell? She's like your first girlfriend, your first kiss – I'll never forget her".

The first Remembrance Day Service after the dedication the previous June was an emotive occasion. The Memorial, highlighted against the November darkness that Sunday evening in 1989.
Cooke

OFFICIAL NAME – WARMWELL

COUNTY	Dorset
LOCATION	4 miles East of Dorchester
LANDMARKS	None
GRID - O/S REF	U193092 - SY765885
LAT/LONG	50 41'40" N 02 20'30" W
HEIGHT ASL	203'
FLYING CONT	Yes
AIRFIELD CODE	P
LIGHTING	Mk. 2
OBSTACLES	Nil

LOCAL NAME – MORETON

LANDING	NE-SW 2700ft Grass
	WNW-ESE 5040ft Grass
	NW-SE 2700ft Grass
HOUSING	Temporary
HANGARS	Bellman - 2
	Blister - 8
OPENED	May 1937
CLOSED	Nov 1945
CURRENT USE	Housing, Holiday Village
	& Quarry

RAF UNITS PRESENT AT WARMWELL

Unit	Codes	From	Date In	Date Out	To	Aircraft Used
6 ATC		(formed	01.05.1937	01.04.1938	(redes. 6 ATS)	Wallace: Tutor
6 ATS		(ex 6 ATC)	01.04.1938	04.09.1939	(redes. CGS)	Wallace: Henley:
						Seal
217 Sqdn.		Tangmere	25.08.1939	02.10.1939	St. Eval	Anson 1
10 AOS		(formed ex 2	03.09.1939	01.11.1939	(redes. 10	Overstrand: Seal
		AOS			B&GS)	Hind: Harrow
10 B&GS		(ex 10 AOS)	01.11.1939	13.07.1940	Dumfries	Various
CGS		(formed)	06.11.1939	25.06.1941	Castle Kennedy	Various
152 Sqdn.	UM	Acklington	12.07.1940	09.04.1941	Portreath	Spitfire 1
13 Sqdn. det.	OO	Hooton Park	07.1940	10.1940	Hooton Park	Lysander
609 Sqdn.	PR	Middle Wallop	29.11.40	24.02.1941	Biggin Hill	Spitfire I
234 Sqdn.	AZ	St. Eval	24.02.1941	05.11.1941	Ibsley	Spitfire V
276 Sqdn. det.	AQ	Harrow beer	21.10.1941	03.04.1944	Portreath	Spitfire: Anson:
						Lysander: Walrus:
						Defiant
402 Sqdn.	AE	Southend	06.11.1941	04.03.1942	Colerne	Hurricane IIb
175 Sqdn.	HH	(formed)	03.03.1942	10.10.1942	Harrow beer	Hurricane IIb
263 Sqdn.	HE	Colerne	13.09.1942	20.02.1943	Harrow beer	Whirlwind I
266 Sqdn.	ZH	Duxford	21.09.1942	02.01.1943	Exeter	Typhoon

257 Sqdn.	FM	Exeter	08.01.1943	12.08.1943	Gravesend	Typhoon 1b
263 Sqdn.	HE	Harrow beer	15.03.1943	19.06.1943	Zeals	Whirlwind I
164 Sqdn.	FJ	Middle Wallop	19.06.1943	05.08.1943	Manston	Hurricane IV
263 Sqdn.	HE	Zeals	12.07.1943	05.12.1943	Ibsley	Whirlwind I
257 Sqdn.	FM	Gravesend	17.09.1943	20.01.1944	Beaulieu	Typhoon I
474th FG,	F5	USA	12.03.1944	06.08.1944	Neuilly (France)	P-38
USAAF	7Y					
	K6					
275 Sqdn.		Valley	14.04.1944	07.08.1944	Bolt Head	Spitfire Vb
277 Sqdn. det.	BA	Shoreham	07.08.1944	18.08.1944	Portreath	Spitfire: Anson:
						Lysander: Walrus:
						Defiant
17 APC		North Weald	08.1944	10.1945	(disbanded)	Martinet: Master:
						Lysander
14 APC		Ayr	11.1944	10.1945	(disbanded)	Martinet: Master:
						Lysander

Note: the above list does not include the multitude of squadrons which visited Warmwell over the years for armament training and practice.

STATION DEFENCE 1940 – 1944

1940 - 1941 RAF General Duties personnel who volunteered for Station Defence Duties, some of which would form the nucleus of 2714 Squadron RAF Regiment

1940 – 1942 The Dorset Regiment, which furnished sections for perimeter defence, including the 70th Young Service Battalion

April 1941 – 1942 2714 Squadron RAF Regiment*

Oct 1942–Oct 1944 2896 Squadron RAF Regiment

1940 – 1941 14th Light Anti-Aircraft Regiment (an Isle of Man TA Unit which dispatched sections to provide anti-aircraft cover to Warmwell and many other south coast airfields)

Numerous other army regiments also retained personnel at Warmwell (many of these troops attended aircraft recognition courses, etc.), were drafted into the defence of the airfield and, on occasions, did engage enemy aircraft.

* During April 1941, volunteer personnel engaged on station defence duties were formed into airfield defence squadrons, but were, as yet, devoid of individual recognition numbers. This was rectified in December of that year. The 150 operational squadrons were formally allocated numbers ranging from 701 onwards but in February 1942 these units were re-designated, prefixing the original number by 2. Thus, 714 Squadron (Warmwell) became 2714 Squadron.

RAF WARMWELL PRESERVATION GROUP

This is the second volume published by the RAF Warmwell Preservation Group as part of its efforts to ensure that the memories of RAF Warmwell are preserved for the future. As such it is a much revised edition. The author has added a considerable amount of new material.

We would like to take this opportunity to acknowledge, with grateful thanks, the contributions of reminiscences that we have received; many of which we have included in this book. We also now have access to a large photographic record of the airfield. Where known, we have included the contributors' names against the photographs. Also, sincere thanks must go to the 474th Fighter Group Association.

The author is a founder member of the Group and has given this work to the project. Together we have, once again, voluntarily prepared the book for publication. All profits from book sales is retained by the Group for the provision of funds for future projects, to chronicle and preserve RAF Warmwell's past.

The Group had considered the establishment of a museum devoted entirely to RAF Warmwell. Sadly, due to financial constraints and other important criteria, these plans have, to date, not been met. The acquisition of specific Warmwell artefacts, which would have formed the nucleus of the display material, has not been achieved to date and, therefore, these plans have been placed on hold. This aspect of the Group's activities has not been forgotten, and work in this direction will continue, albeit at a much reduced pace.

In the meantime, plans are being made to erect a plaque at Holy Trinity Church, Warmwell, which was the local church to the airfield, in remembrance of the personnel from RAF Warmwell.

Today, very little trace of the former airfield is evident to the casual observer. One would need to have an eagle eye, and an interest in military architecture, to realise that, at some time in the past, a military base was established in and around what is now the village of Crossways.

As people pass away, their memories and their associated history is lost forever - *because it is people who make history.* The story of those who served and survived is as important as those who made the supreme sacrifice. Sadly, within a few years, all traces of RAF Warmwell may have disappeared, for the few buildings that do remain are under threat as time marches on and homes are built for today's generation.

The RAF Warmwell Preservation Group will strive to preserve and record the annals, heritage and memory of the airfield and its dramatic history.

Visit our website – http://www.rafwarmwell.org.uk

Contact us at – info@rafwarmwell.org.uk

Website design by Mike of Finding The Time

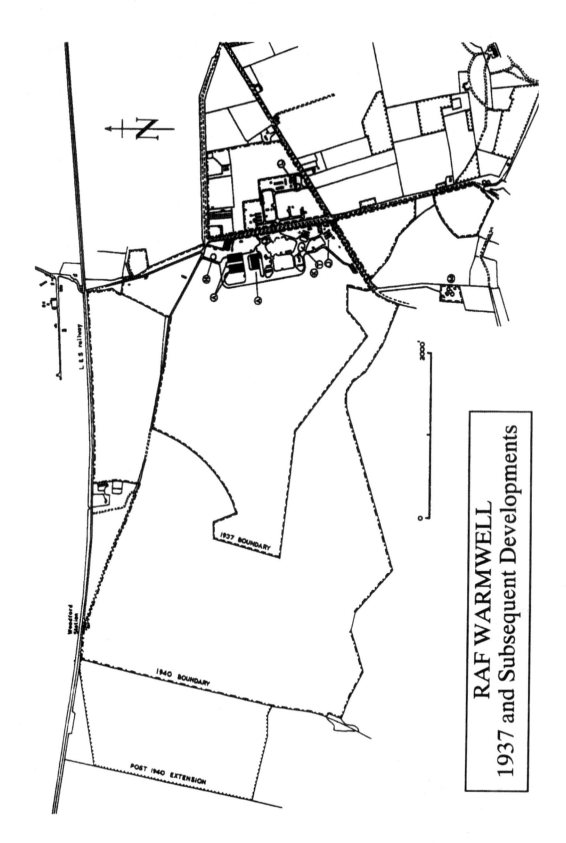

RAF WARMWELL
1937 and Subsequent Developments

1937 BOUNDARY

1940 BOUNDARY

POST 1940 EXTENSION

L & S railway

Woodford Station

N

2000

0

RAF Warmwell viewed from the west. (Courtesy J. Hamlin)

Ground staff pose with a Miles Martenet target towing aircraft in their care, from one of the Armament Practice Camp units operating at Warmwell.
Cooke/Mason

Whoops!
K6773 of 62 Squadron overshot the airfield boundary and flipped over on to its upper wing.
Cooke/Cronk